After Prisons?

After Prisons?

Freedom, Decarceration, and Justice Disinvestment

Edited by
William G. Martin and Joshua M. Price

LEXINGTON BOOKS
Lanham • Boulder • New York • London

Published by Lexington Books
An imprint of The Rowman & Littlefield Publishing Group, Inc.
4501 Forbes Boulevard, Suite 200, Lanham, Maryland 20706
www.rowman.com

Unit A, Whitacre Mews, 26-34 Stannary Street, London SE11 4AB

British Library Cataloguing in Publication Information Available

Library of Congress Cataloging-in-Publication Data
Names: Martin, William G., 1952- editor. | Price, Joshua M., editor.
Title: After prisons? : freedom, decarceration, and justice disinvestment / edited by William G. Martin and Joshua M. Price.
Description: Lanham : Lexington Books, [2016] | Includes bibliographical references and index.
Identifiers: LCCN 2016023403 (print) | LCCN 2016027357 (ebook) | ISBN 9781498539159 (cloth : alk. paper) | ISBN 9781498539166 (electronic)
Subjects: LCSH: Prisons—New York (State) | Corrections—New York (State) | Criminal justice, Administration of—New York (State)
Classification: LCC HV9475.N7 A48 2016 (print) | LCC HV9475.N7 (ebook) | DDC 364.809747—dc23
LC record available at https://lccn.loc.gov/2016023403

∞™ The paper used in this publication meets the minimum requirements of American National Standard for Information Sciences—Permanence of Paper for Printed Library Materials, ANSI/NISO Z39.48-1992.

Printed in the United States of America

Dedicated to the memory of Herman Wallace, Sandra Bland, and all those many others who came before, and who are with us yet, who improvise upon our vision of the future.

Contents

Acknowledgments

The authors wish to thank the Dean of Harpur College, Binghamton University, who generously supported speakers series on decarceration and policing; Binghamton University's Citizenship, Rights and Cultural Belonging Transdisciplinary Area of Excellence project, which provided a seed grant; Reuben Miller who inspired and graciously commented on our work; and Carissa Marcelle and Brighid Stone of Lexington Books who patiently and skillfully shepherded the manuscript to publication. We would also like to thank our colleagues and comrades in Binghamton, as well as the New York State Prisoner Justice Network, whose members exemplified the civic participation to which we aspire.

Introduction

From Mass Imprisonment to Decarceration and Justice Disinvestment

William G. Martin

The student was angry and emphatic: "The prisons they're building? They are already planning places to put our kids and grandkids there." Sitting in a classroom in one of New York's maximum security prisons, the student had personally experienced how a veritable prison archipelago had arisen in the closing decades of the twentieth century. In the early 1970s fewer than 200,000 persons were incarcerated in state and federal prisons; by the year 2000 the number had reached over 1.5 million, with 7 million under some form of criminal justice supervision (prison, jail, parole, probation). This was incarceration on an unsurpassed scale, with the United States exceeding rates reached in the Soviet Union, China, and, for black men, apartheid South Africa. The overwhelmingly black and brown classroom that day represented as well a highly racialized and spatially-stratified system, stretching across the poor and segregated urban and rural communities of New York State. Scholars at the turn of the century offered the same conclusion as the young black student: mass imprisonment had become an entrenched feature of the social landscape of the country and a central pillar of the post-welfare, neoliberal state (Beckett and Western 2001; D. Garland 2002). Mass imprisonment, it was widely agreed, had no limits to its future.

In the last five years this conclusion has been rudely shaken. Nationwide, the number of people incarcerated has plateaued and in a few states, most notably New York, sharply declined. This unexpected development has been accompanied by a sea change in political discourse as fiscal conservatives have united with liberal governors of Northeastern states and conservative Southwestern states to champion a downsizing of the nation's prison complex. Criminal justice policy reform has been widely promoted and celebrated. In 2013, then-Attorney-General Eric Holder called for a repeal of some of the harshest sentencing laws of the war on drugs, and key states began to roll back draconian drug laws and prison conditions, and roll out alternatives to incarceration.

These outcomes have been long in coming. The long-standing efforts of prisoner support movements, networks (e.g., the New York State Prisoner Justice Network) and campaigns (e.g., Drop the Rock) have been supplemented in recent years by more organized and better funded advocacy groups and institutions. These are close to achieving key goals, including legislation easing the strict conditions for parole (e.g., the Riverside Church Campaign to End Parole Abuses and Reunite Families [http://www.parolereformnow.org]), curtailing the use of prison isolation units (the Campaign for Alternatives to Isolated Confinement [http://nycaic.org/]), and raising the age at which youth are tried as adults (the Raise the Age NY campaign [http://raisetheageny.com/]).[1] Many nonprofit organizations engaged in prisoner and reentry support work, from the Osborne Association and the Fortune Society to the Correctional Association, have also pushed hard in this direction. At the same time more radical protest by abolitionist organizations such as Critical Resistance, it must be noticed, has been eclipsed by more professionalized advocacy and nonprofit organizations (Gilmore 2015). By 2016, however, a new consensus appears to emerging from the White House, through state houses, to the op-ed pages of the country's media: a new era of criminal justice reform is upon us.

While welcome, such a conclusion rests on hopes and not observations of the extent or impact of decarceration. In the 1970s, similar expectations of closing the nation's prisons were raised in the wake of mass protest and fiscal crisis, only to be followed by the era of mass incarceration. What kind of future do today's events and pronouncements signal? Do the first signs of decarceration signal the dismantling of mass incarceration—and the new era of social justice for which so many of us have struggled? We do not know: there is little published research on the recent wave of decarceration.

This book aims to begin to provide answers to these questions.

FROM MASS INCARCERATION TO TENTATIVE DECARCERATION

Histories and theories of the rise of mass incarceration invariably focus on factors that sustain continued high levels of incarceration. Much work has been done: criminologists and public policy advocates have expended substantial effort to counter widespread myths regarding mass imprisonment. Targeted in particular is the crime-fighting narrative publicized by the media, politicians, and many conservative policy analysts and scholars, namely that as crime accelerated in the 1970s and 1980s, laws were toughened up, criminals were sent down, and crime rates obligingly fell. Considerable data and correlations exist to reject such simplistic explanations (e.g., Western 2006, and more circumspectly the recent survey by the National Research Council [2014]). Crime rates have at best a weak relation to imprisonment rates and the highly racialized and gendered composition of the millions warehoused in the nation's jails and prisons. The sources of mass incarceration have more convincingly been traced to a crime panic propagated by the mass media, and the abandonment in the 1970s by radicals, liberals, and conservatives alike of the post-war rehabilitative ideal (Mauer 1999, 42–48; Murakawa 2014; Wacquant 2009, 7–11; Western 2006, 59–62).

As suggested by the concept of a "prison industrial complex" (Davis 2003; Gilmore 2007), mass incarceration was accompanied by a broader, long-term transition away from a liberal, social democratic state to an increasingly less democratic and burgeoning "carceral" state. Central here was the weak and shrinking welfare state under neoliberalism, and the imposition of a workfare and incarcerating state (Gottschalk 2015, 87–90; Wacquant 2009, 58–69). Those more closely attuned to social and empirical data stress a parallel outcome: the entrenchment of mass imprisonment deep in the country's social and economic life. In Bruce Western's words, mass imprisonment had become "self-sustaining," ensuring that "the penal system will remain as it has become, a significant feature on the new landscape of American poverty and race relations" (2006, 198).

The prospect of decarceration unsettles these conclusions and the certainty of unobstructed, continued mass incarceration as we have known it for almost two generations. It also demands a new framework to understand the changes before us. This book, based on over three years of original ethnographic, historical, and statistical research across New York State, begins to chart a fitful reconfiguration of the criminal justice complex. Our conclusion is demonstrably *not* the one envisioned by reformers, namely a rational shrinking of the carceral archipelago and the construction of a more just and rehabilitative system in its place. Nor is it one predicated on a continuation of mass incarceration.

Instead, our findings suggest a far more geographically diverse and complicated process of *justice disinvestment* as the state *devolves* direct responsibility for the operation of the criminal justice system to local authorities and the nonprofit sector, and yet seeks to extend its reach through coordinating new forms of community-based supervision, surveillance and policing. The uncritical celebration of criminal justice reform is thus at best premature and at worst obscures the forces at work. Far from retreating, our research indicates that the state has moved to insert itself ever deeper into the very communities from which most incarcerated persons come—further impoverishing and disenfranchising both rural and urban communities.

DECARCERATION: NEW YORK

New York State is a signal location to investigate what mass incarceration produced. New York has been a harbinger of criminal justice reform and innovation since building the first modern prisons nearly two hundred years ago. Major reform movements in New York State throughout the nineteenth and twentieth centuries left their mark across the country, as did new punitive policies launched in the wake of the 1971 Attica rebellion. New York was one of the first to impose harsh sentencing in the war on drugs in the 1970s, and was one of the first states to begin large-scale construction of new prisons in the 1980s. Mass incarceration and its parallel policing and legal components were very much part of the New York state of mind in the 1980s and 1990s.

In the last ten years New York State has now fueled expectations for significant decarceration: the number of adults in the state's prisons has dropped by over 25 percent and continues downward as Figure I.1 indicates.

This has led to the closing of sixteen adult prisons since 2009. Doors have been shuttered on over thirty juvenile prisons (officially designed

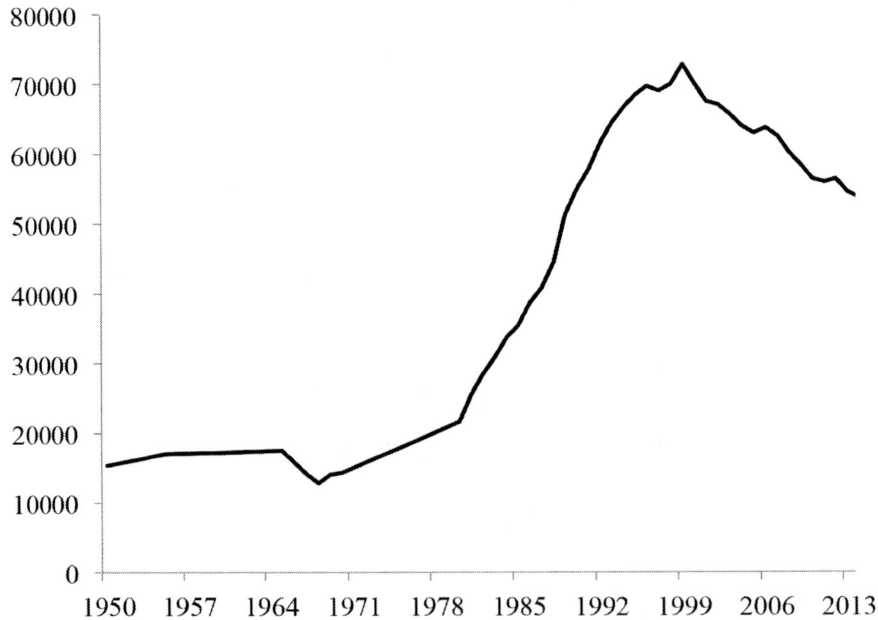

Figure I.1 Incarcerated: NYS Prisons 1950–2014. *Source*: Data from Hindelang, Dunn, Sutton, Aumick 1970: 351 (for 1950–1970); United States, Bureau of Justice Statistics data (for 1977–2002), http://www.bjs.gov/index.cfm?ty=tp&tid=1#data_collections; and New York State, Department of Corrections and Community Supervision data (for 2007–2014), http://www.doccs.ny.gov/Research/annotate.html#cjstats.

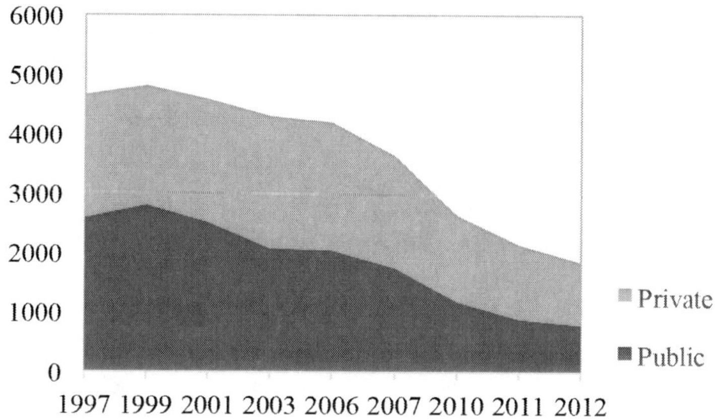

Figure I.2 New York: Youth in Public and Private Facilities. *Source*: Data from Sickmund et al. 2013; U.S. Department of Justice 2015.

as "detention" or "residential" centers) as well, with the number of youth imprisoned in both private and state facilities falling by over 60 percent as indicated in Figure I.2.

New York City's jail population has similarly fallen from a peak daily average of over 22,000 in the early 1990s to 10,000 on an average day in 2015 (though the jail population has grown elsewhere, as we argue below). Many expect these changes to continue, producing a smaller, more humane, and more just criminal justice system.

NATIONAL DECARCERATION?

New York State has not been alone. By 2010, signs of the attenuation and even reversal of mass incarceration were appearing across the country. In 2008, the national imprisonment rate declined for the first time in decades, and in the next year the number of persons in the United States under correctional control—on probation, parole, or in prisons and jails—receded for the first time since the Bureau of Justice began reporting comprehensive statistics in 1980. By 2014 thirty-nine states were reporting declines in their prison populations, with twelve states reporting double-digit falls (The Sentencing Project 2016). California, under court orders to reduce its inhumanely overcrowded prisons, reported a 22 percent retreat from its 2006 record high.

Reform-minded journalists, policymakers, and op-ed writers have widely celebrated these changes. Writing a cover story for *The Nation*, Sasha

Abramsky, author of *Conned* (2006), celebrated how the "perpetual prisoner machine" was getting "gummed up" as "for the first time in more than forty years, criminal justice trends are starting to move in a sensible direction" (2010, 15–16). A new wave of sentencing reform seemed to push in this direction, most notably through attempts to cut back long-term, mandatory sentences for drug offenses. The Congressional passage of the Fair Sentencing Act of 2010, which reduced the crack: powder cocaine sentencing disparity from 100:1 to 18:1, was matched by similar legislation in many states. The establishment of special drug courts, more lenient parole policies, and more community-based alternatives to incarceration mark for many the beginnings of a less punitive, more rational criminal justice system.

JUSTICE REINVESTMENT

"Justice Reinvestment" has been the most prominent attempt to move in this direction by pairing a reduction in prison budgets to investments in high-incarceration communities (Austin et al. 2013; Greene et al. 2010; Tucker and Cadora 2003). This potentially includes not only new support for reentry, health, job training, and social services for the formerly incarcerated, but also new investments in education, housing, and employment. Promoted by foundations, nonprofits and scholars, Justice Reinvestment has been launched in over twenty-seven states by a coalition including the Council of State Governments and the JFA Institute, with support from the Open Society Institute and more recently the Pew Charitable Trusts and the Bureau of Justice Assistance. Attorney General Eric Holder, speaking at the American Bar Association in 2013, applauded the states, governors and legislators of both parties who had "directed funding away from prison construction and toward evidence-based programs and services, like treatment and supervision that are designed to reduce recidivism." "Reinvestment and serious reform," Holder argued, "are improving public safety and saving precious resources" (2013).

Assessments of progress to date have become far more tentative however with the two key pillars of Justice Reinvestment left unrealized: after a three year decline, the number of persons incarcerated nationwide began to rise again in 2013, while grand proposals to reinvest savings into reentry and community services have failed to materialize. As the original proponents of justice reinvestment concede: "If the goal is to reduce mass incarceration, there is scant evidence of success. More alarming, there is little indication that historic rates of incarceration will be reduced in the future" (Austin et al. 2013, 11). Senior scholars and activists have been blunter, reasserting the endurance of mass incarceration (Gottschalk 2015, 259; Kilgore 2014).

Despite the Great Recession's considerable pressure on state budgets, decarceration has clearly not taken off across the country.

GEOGRAPHIES OF DECARCERATION

Are recent trends in New York thus an anomaly? Few doubt that New York State has served as a national model for mass incarceration, and New York City as the model for related policing innovations under New York Police Department Chief Bratton and Mayor Giuliani in the 1990s. Yet it is equally evident that New York State's criminal justice patterns have diverged quite significantly from those of the South or even from demographically similar states in the North, Midwest, or West. In recent years scholars have become far more attentive to how local histories and the concrete relations among states have shaped the incarceration boom in the United States and the world (Eason 2010; Lynch 2010; Perkinson 2010).

These observations serve to move us beyond grand narratives that circumscribe mass incarceration to crime rates, moral panics, and the study of the prison and the ghettos from which the incarcerated come (Wacquant 2001). Decarceration promises to disrupt however the much larger network of social control mechanisms that entangles the actions of the governor and multiple state departments, police and intelligence forces, parole and county welfare agencies, prison administrators, and mayors from New York City to small towns along the border with Canada. To concentrate only upon New York City as a model for the state or country misses precisely what has been created over three decades: an incarcerating complex that links together social and economic life all across the state.

The major geographic and political poles of this network are most commonly depicted as conservative, small town and rural "upstate" New York and its opposite, "downstate" New York, centered on liberal New York City.[2] The terms are ubiquitous and act to stigmatize the "rural," a term that has long troubled scholars (Bell 2007). What qualifies as "upstate" and "downstate" has also shifted as the social and political economy of the state has changed over time, most notably when major manufacturing firms upstate collapsed after World War II and New York City's recent emergence as a global financial and tourist center. Mass incarceration also made its contribution to the widening inequality between New York City and impoverished rural communities, as tens of thousands of persons convicted in New York City's courts were dispatched to the distant prisons in the poor North. This phenomenon is stereotypically cast as rural white towns getting rich at the expense of the big city's black and Latino populations, defaming both (see Eason 2017).

If mass incarceration served to further concentrate and link zones of wealth and power, decarceration as it evolves is not following past constructions of upstate vs. downstate. As the following chapters chart, prisons have closed in *both* small towns "upstate" and in large cities "downstate." Almost half the persons released from incarceration return to "upstate" communities and *not* just New York City. The current media and political war on drugs marks *upstate* communities most fiercely. And incarceration is *expanding* upstate even as it declines downstate. New York State is as marked by different rates and paths of incarceration and decarceration as the country is as a whole.

Decarceration has not even led to the most expected outcome: cost savings. Many calling for reform have argued in the wake of 2007 Great Recession that fiscal crises are good moments to push substantive reforms and prison downsizing (Clear 2011; Garland et al. 2014). Historians are less certain (Gottschalk 2011a; Gottschalk 2011b, 484–85). Falling state revenues due to the recession and the necessity to balance state budgets (unlike the federal ability to run large deficits) have certainly directed governors' attention to the cost of the penal and policing arms of the state. And contrary to depictions of their invincibility, powerful statewide public employee unions have not been able to prevent prison closings, despite protests and ongoing media advertising campaigns across New York. As a harbinger of things to come, the most vigorous applause in Governor Andrew Cuomo's first State of the State address in 2011 was when he loudly proclaimed "An incarceration program is not an employment program" (Hakim and Confessore 2011).

As the data above document, the contraction of the prison system predates the Great Recession and now continues in New York, as in other states, despite recent, unexpected budget surpluses due to rising general tax revenues as many states recover from the Great Recession (Lyman 2014). If in the 1980s and 1990s states invested in mass incarceration to boost their economies by putting to work surplus land, labor, and capital (Gilmore 1998; 2007), this dynamic seems to no longer hold. Economic pump-priming by expanding state spending on the prison complex, or "carceral Keynesianism," is giving way to a smaller state that decarcerates.

PATHS OF DECARCERATION AND DEVOLUTION

The prospect of a smaller state raises the widespread possibility of what Miller (2014) documents for reentry programming in Chicago, where "devolution" takes place as state policies "transfer carceral authority—in this case the authority to rehabilitate and supervise prisoners—from federal and state-based institutions to local ones. . . . Geographically, rehabilitation has been outsourced and privatized, moving from within prison walls and into the therapeutic spaces, church basements, and community centers of the inner city" (Miller 2014, 308). In this manner the supervisory state reaches further into the neighborhood, streets, and families of the formerly and yet-to-be-incarcerated poor. Decarceration and devolution may thus shape our future in ways unexpected by the states' and criminologists' narrow concern with returning incarcerated persons to their home communities.

Reform is also being directed into quite sharply defined channels. Most reformers now restrict sentencing and parole reforms to those convicted of the three "nons": the non-violent, non-serious, and non-sexual offenses (Gottschalk 2015, 165–95). The drop in the number of persons newly committed to state prisons has largely been due to fewer drug and low-level felony arrests and convictions, particularly from New York City. The number of imprisoned drug offenders dropped from 24,085 in 1996 to 7,053 in 2012 (New York State Department of Corrections and Community Supervision 2013). Of the 53,000 persons incarcerated in New York's prisons in late 2014, fewer than 7,000 persons were there for drug offenses. This shows the limits of reform, lending credence to those who foresee the continuation of mass incarceration: even if remaining drug offenders were to be released, and new admissions were correlated to falling crime rate, New York State would still have over 30,000 persons in its prisons.

Incarceration has also become more punitive for those remaining in the system: of the sixteen adult prisons closed since 2009, all were medium and minimum security prisons including many drug and addiction treatment centers. State juvenile detention centers are now almost exclusively "secure" detention facilities. Evidence suggests that remaining prisons and jails have become overcrowded, leading to claims by the correctional officers' union that overcrowded, "double-bunked" prisons have created dangerous conditions. Violence and corruption at New York City's massive Rikers Island jail, despite its now much smaller population, has led to a series of public investigations and unsuccessful reforms.

These developments suggest less rehabilitative and harsher terms of imprisonment as decarceration proceeds. Tracing the paths of the over 20,000 persons released from prisons each year lends further evidence for this. Until quite recently, reentry services have for over fifty years had minimal support from most states and cities. The voluntary agencies that provided services in the past clearly lacked the resources to deal with the new flow of people out of prisons. These agencies are primarily based in New York City, moreover, leaving upstate New York with far fewer resources than it needs to assist the 42 percent of the state's prison population who come from and return to upstate counties (State of New York Department of Corrections and Community Supervision 2013, 6).

Numerous new reentry and alternative-to-incarceration (ATI) programs have been announced by state and city agencies. They are largely implemented through nonprofit agencies, community-based organizations, the corporate sector, and local policing and probation organizations, giving rise to what some have called a non-profit-industrial complex (Incite! Women of Color Against Violence 2007). Nonprofit organizations working in the criminal justice area have proliferated. New York State nonprofits working in and around the criminal justice system have grown rapidly: between 1995 and 2010 the number of registered nonprofits in the crime and legal area in New York State grew by 40 percent and revenues doubled; the number of registered nonprofits specializing in rehabilitation services for offenders tripled.[3] Larger organizations like the Osborne Association and the Fortune Society have seen their revenues double as well, as post-prison services have increasingly been delegated by the state to the nonprofit sector. Devolution of programming and supervision to the non-state agencies has been matched to a drive by the state to coordinate the expansion of such programs throughout the state through reentry task forces. What the state has *not* done is significantly expand its own parole or probation efforts as indicated in Figure I.3 which shows a fall in the number of adults on parole and probation.

The number of parole and full-time police officers has also dropped in recent years. When matched to the transfer of responsibility for juvenile detention and treatment to private centers, this reveals another aspect of significant carceral devolution: a shrinking state sector offset by the growing supervision through the private sector at the local, community level. There is

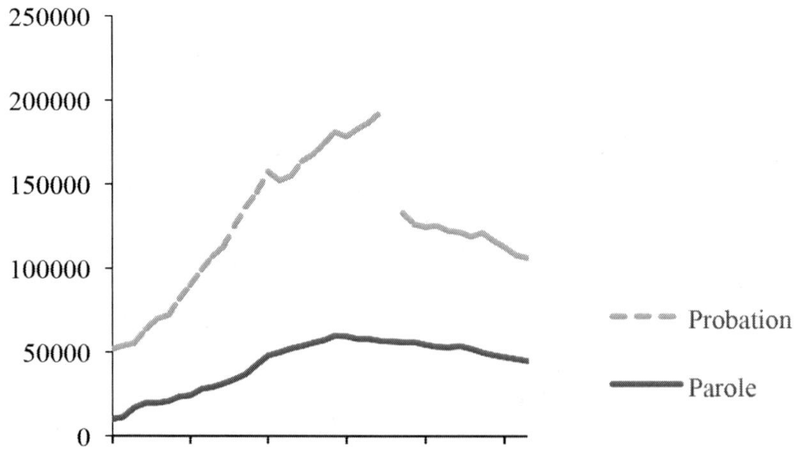

Figure I.3 NYS: Parole and Probation 1977–2013. *Note*: Probation data reporting methods changed in 2002. *Source*: Data from Bureau of Justice Statistics. Parole: http://www.bjs.gov/index.cfm?ty=pbdetail&iid=2026. Probation: http://www.bjs.gov/index.cfm?ty=pbdetail&iid=1997.

little prospect under these conditions of rolling back the stigmatization and civic isolation, or *social death* as Price details it (2015), imposed upon the incarcerated and formerly incarcerated alike.

LOOKING FORWARD: JUSTICE DISINVESTMENT

If we are to move forward to less incarceration and greater social justice, we urgently need to make sense of the conflicting expectations, policies, projections and data surrounding the sudden flurry of talk surrounding criminal justice reform. Five years ago we began as a group to sense—due to our advocacy in prisons, jails, reentry, and local justice projects—cracks in the stability and immutability of the mass incarceration complex. We then formed a collective research group to investigate these cracks or fissures. Our research and advocacy reflected our location in Binghamton, a small rust-belt town in central New York surrounded by prisons to the west, central, and northern reaches of New York State. As our work progressed we gradually added colleagues working in the South and Midwest.

As our discussions moved forward we shifted our investigation beyond the confines of the great prisons and large cities upon which our models have been built. This meant moving from rural prison towns to the home communities of incarcerated and formerly incarcerated persons. The following chapters explore, across the uneven carceral geography of New York, the impact of closing prisons, uneven shifts in media coverage of drug wars and incarceration, the coordination of new forms of reentry programming utilizing "risk-based metrics," the diverging dynamics of state prisons and local jails, and the entrenchment of intelligence-led policing and parole.

In all these areas we find halting movement by the state toward the ever-sharper coordination of criminal justice operations, even as the state shifts supervision and incarceration increasingly onto the private and nonprofit sector. In projecting the future my incarcerated student, fearing the building of yet more prisons for children and grandchildren yet to come, may have only slightly miscalculated. Prisons may close, but reform may all too easily displace our hopes for greater social justice into private and unseen areas.

NOTES

1. New York tries as adults all 16- and 17-year-old youth charged with a crime, one of only two states to do so. New York also treats 13-, 14-, and 15-year-olds accused of committing certain serious crimes as "juvenile offenders," and prosecutes them as adults unless their cases are transferred to Family Court. All 16- and 17-year-olds detained or incarcerated via a criminal court order are confined in adult prisons and

jails; juvenile offenders are confined in youth facilities until at least 18. These age limits are likely to be changed shortly by new legislation.

2. The terms "upstate" and "downstate" are defined differently by multiple state agencies, the media, and social and economic analysts. New York City and its nearby suburbs (and occasionally some "exurbs" on rail lines) and Long Island are almost always considered "downstate." Those living in the "Far North," near the Canadian border where many prisons were erected in the 1980s and 1990s, often reject the use of the term "upstate" to reference even rural western or central New York—as one state assembly woman from the far North firmly corrected the author's use of the term in a meeting on parole and prison legislation reform. For an illustration see the maps and discussion in several chapters below.

3. These figures and those in the next sentence are from "NCCS All Registered Nonprofits," National Center for Charitable Statistics, available from http://nccsweb.urban.org/tablewiz/bmf.php (accessed October 13, 2014). They only cover non-profits that register and file with the IRS in these categories and are thus very rough approximations.

REFERENCES

Abramsky, Sasha. 2006. *Conned: How Millions Went to Prison, Lost the Vote, and Helped Send George W. Bush to the White House*. New York: New Press.

———. 2010. "Is This the End of the War on Crime?" *The Nation* 291 (1): 11–16.

Austin, James, Eric Cadora, Todd R. Clear, Kara Dansky, Judith Greene, Vanita Gupta, Marc Mauer, Nicole Porter, Susan Tucker, and Malcolm C. Young. 2013. "Ending Mass Incarceration: Charting a New Justice Reinvestment." ACLU, Justice Strategies, Sentencing Project. http://sentencingproject.org/doc/publications/sen_Charting%20a%20New%20Justice%20Reinvestment.pdf. Accessed April 1, 2014.

Beckett, Katherine, and Bruce Western. 2001. "Governing Social Marginality: Welfare, Incarceration, and the Transformation of State Policy." *Punishment & Society* 3 (1): 43–59. doi:10.1177/14624740122228249.

Bell, Michael M. 2007. "The Two-Ness of Rural Life and the Ends of Rural Scholarship." *Journal of Rural Studies* 23 (4): 402–15. doi:10.1016/j.jrurstud.2007.03.003.

Clear, Todd R. 2011. "A Private-Sector, Incentives-Based Model for Justice Reinvestment: Justice Reinvestment." *Criminology & Public Policy* 10 (3): 585–608. doi:10.1111/j.1745-9133.2011.00729.x.

Davis, Angela Y. 2003. *Are Prisons Obsolete?* New York: Seven Stories Press.

Eason, John. 2010. "Mapping Prison Proliferation: Region, Rurality, Race and Disadvantage in Prison Placement." *Social Science Researc*h 39 (6): 1015–28. doi:10.1016/j.ssresearch.2010.03.001.

———. Forthcoming 2017. *Big House on the Prairie: Rise of the Rural Ghetto & Prison Proliferation*. Chicago: University of Chicago Press.

Garland, Brett, Nancy Hogan, Eric Wodahl, Aida Hass, Marry K. Stohr, and Eric Lambert. 2014. "Decarceration and Its Possible Effects on Inmates, Staff, and Communities." *Punishment & Society* 16 (4): 448–73. doi:10.1177/1462474514539535.

Garland, David. 2002. *The Culture of Control: Crime and Social Order in Contemporary Society*. Chicago: University of Chicago Press.

Gilmore, Ruth Wilson. 1998. "Globalisation and US Prison Growth: From Military Keynesianism to Post-Keynesian Militarism." *Race & Class* 40 (2/3): 171–88.

———. 2007. *Golden Gulag: Prisons, Surplus, Crisis, and Opposition in Globalizing California*. Berkeley: University of California Press.

———. 2015. "The Worrying State of the Anti-Prison Movement." *Social Justice*, February. http://www.socialjusticejournal.org/the-worrying-state-of-the-anti-prison-movement/.

Gottschalk, Marie. 2011a. "The Great Recession and the Great Confinement: The Economic Crisis and the Future of Penal Reform." In *Contemporary Issues in Criminological Theory and Research: The Role of Social Institutions*, edited by Richard Rosenfeld, Kenna Quinet, and Crystal Garcia, 343–70. Belmont, CA: Wadsworth/Cengage.

———. 2011b. "The Past, Present, and Future of Mass Incarceration in the United States: Special Issue." *Criminology & Public Policy* 10 (3): 483–504. doi:10.1111/j.1745-9133.2011.00755.x.

———. 2015. *Caught: The Prison State and the Lockdown of American Politics*. Princeton: Princeton University Press.

Greene, Judith A., Marc Mauer, Justice Strategies, and N. Y. Brooklyn. 2010. *Downscaling Prisons: Lessons from Four States*. Sentencing Project.

Hakim, Danny, and Nicholas Confessore. 2011. "Speech Suggests Pro-Business Approach by Cuomo." *New York Times*, January 5. http://www.nytimes.com/2011/01/06/nyregion/06cuomo.html?pagewanted=all&_r=0. Accessed July 3, 2014.

Hindelang, Michael J., Cristopher S. Dunn, Paul Sutton, and Alison L. Aumick. 1970. *Sourcebook of Criminal Justice Statistics, 1970*. Washington, DC: U.S. Department of Justice.

Holder, Eric. 2013. "Attorney General Eric Holder Delivers Remarks at the Annual Meeting of the American Bar Association's House of Delegates." United States Department of Justice. http://www.justice.gov/iso/opa/ag/speeches/2013/ag-speech-130812.html. Accessed October 24, 2014.

Incite! Women of Color Against Violence, ed. 2007. *The Revolution Will Not Be Funded: Beyond the Non-Profit Industrial Complex*. Cambridge, MA: South End Press.

Kilgore, James. 2014. "The Persistence of Mass Incarceration." *Counterpunch*, September. http://www.counterpunch.org/2014/09/23/the-persistence-of-mass-incarceration/. Accessed October 6, 2014.

Lyman, Rick. 2014. "Battles Looming Over Surpluses in Many States." *New York Times*, February 2.

Lynch, Mona Pauline. 2010. *Sunbelt Justice: Arizona and the Transformation of American Punishment*. Critical Perspectives on Crime and Law. Stanford, CA: Stanford Law Books.

Mauer, Marc. 1999. *Race to Incarcerate*. New York: New Press: Distributed by W.W. Norton.

Miller, Reuben J. 2014. "Devolving the Carceral State: Race, Prisoner Reentry, and the Micro-Politics of Urban Poverty Management." *Punishment & Society* 16 (3): 305–35. doi:10.1177/1462474514527487.

Murakawa, Naomi. 2014. *The First Civil Right: How Liberals Built Prison America.* New York: Oxford University Press.

National Research Council (U.S.). 2014. *The Growth of Incarceration in the United States: Exploring Causes and Consequences.* Edited by Jeremy Travis and Bruce Western. Washington, DC: The National Academies Press.

New York State. Department of Corrections and Community Supervision. 2013. "The New York State Department of Corrections and Community Supervision Announces Prison Reforms That Will Save Taxpayers Over $30 Million Annually Following Decline in Crime Rate and Inmate Population." Albany, NY. http://www.doccs.ny.gov/PressRel/2013/Prison_Closure_Announcement.html. Accessed July 6, 2014.

Perkinson, Robert. 2010. *Texas Tough: The Rise of America's Prison Empire.* New York: Metropolitan Books.

Price, Joshua M. 2015. *Prison and Social Death.* New Brunswick, NJ: Rutgers University Press.

Sickmund, Melissa, Anthony Sladky, W. Kang, and C. Puzzanchera. 2013. "Easy Access to the Census of Juveniles in Residential Placement." www.ojjdp.gov/ojstatbb/ezacjrp.

State of New York. Department of Corrections and Community Supervision. 2013. "Under Custody Report: Profile of Inmate Population under Custody on January 1, 2013." www.doccs.ny.gov/Research/Reports/2014/UnderCustody_Report_2014.pdf. Accessed March 6, 2016.

The Sentencing Project. 2016. "U.S. Prison Population Trends 1999–2014." http://www.sentencingproject.org/detail/publication.cfm?publication_id=602&id=156. Accessed March 10, 2016.

Tucker, Susan, and Eric Cadora. 2003. "Justice Reinvestment: To Invest in Public Safety by Reallocating Justice Dollars to Refinance Education, Housing, Healthcare, and Jobs." *Ideas for an Open Society* 3 (3): 2–5.

United States Department of Justice. Bureau of Justice Statistics. 2011. "Prisoners in 2009." http://bjs.ojp.usdoj.gov/index.cfm?ty=pbdetail&iid=2232. Accessed March 26, 2014.

———. 2015. "Prisoners in 2014." http://www.bjs.gov/index.cfm?ty=pbdetail&iid=5387. Accessed March 1, 2016.

United States Department of Justice. Office of Justice Programs. Office of Juvenile Justice and Delinquency Prevention. 2015. "Juvenile Residential Facility Census, 2012: Selected Findings." http://www.ojjdp.gov/pubs/247207.pdf. Accessed January 15, 2016.

Wacquant, Loïc. 2001. "Deadly Symbiosis: When Ghetto and Prison Meet and Mesh." *Punishment & Society* 3 (1): 95–133. doi:10.1177/14624740122228276.

———. 2009. *Punishing the Poor: The Neoliberal Government of Social Insecurity.* Durham, NC: Duke University Press.

Western, Bruce. 2006. *Punishment and Inequality in America.* New York: R. Sage Foundation.

Chapter 1

The Prison Town Boom and Bust in the Empire State[1]

William G. Martin, John Major Eason, and Luis R. Gonzalez

Asked what would happen if the historic prison on the outskirts of his town were to close, the mayor was blunt: "It would kill us." The prison had, he continued, provided employment for generations who "walked up the hill" to work, day after day, year after year (Casale 2014). While franker than most, he was not alone—this was a sentiment repeated by mayors and community officials in interviews across New York State. And therein lies the hidden history of the states' prison archipelago. For behind the fortress prison and its incarcerated individuals lies a wide, forbidding landscape entangling the lives of the rural and urban, poor and rich, powerful and powerless. This chapter tackles the fate of the forgotten towns where prisons were built during the mass imprisonment era and where, most unexpectedly, prisons are now closing.

New York State is a good place to study the meaning of decarceration for prison towns: the state has long been renowned for its carceral innovations. The celebrity of the first modern, silent, and rehabilitative prisons at Auburn and Sing Sing attracted many visitors in the early nineteenth century, most notably Alexis de Tocqueville in the summer of 1832; their early disciplinary practices provided the foundation for Foucault's much later work (1977). The modern reformatory movement, based on classification and occupational training, was inaugurated by the Elmira prison in 1876 and the international conference held to highlight and disperse Elmira's achievements. Almost a century later a brutal carceral and criminal justice wave would follow the Attica revolt of 1971, with the state in the late 1970s building new prisons and expanding old ones. By the end of the century New York would imprison 73,000 people, a dramatic leap from the 14,000 in prison in 1970. Nationwide, over 1,100 facilities would be constructed as part of the boom from 1970 to 2000.

At the dawn of the twenty-first century New York appears to be leading the country again, but this time in reducing mass imprisonment and closing prisons. But what do these tentative steps towards decarceration portend for the towns that host prisons? As the mayor's comments suggest, prison building is widely asserted to be a zero-sum game with white, rural communities reaping profits at the expense of poor, urban, minority communities (Alexander 2010; Gilmore 2007; Huling 2002; Schlosser 1998). As Tracy Huling argues for New York, "the use of prisons as money-makers for struggling rural communities has become a major force driving criminal justice policy toward mass incarceration of the urban poor" (2002, 213). And indeed of the thirty-nine state prisons built after 1980 in New York, twenty-three were located in non-metropolitan areas. From these developments it is easy to construct a narrative of white rural communities not just benefitting from but propelling the incarceration of urban black and brown people.

Our research shows that this narrative holds for neither the nation nor New York State. Prison proliferation linked the poor and marginalized peoples of rural and urban communities in a deadly embrace. The pattern of prison closings now threatens to destabilize and further impoverish both, as new centers of wealth have emerged around the global financial center of New York City and the state shifts investment from the public to private sector. In short: the political economy of decarceration promises yet further economic and social polarization within and among the cities and peoples of New York.

We proceed in three steps. First, we briefly evaluate the state of knowledge regarding prison towns. Second, we examine more closely the New York State pattern, contextualizing and charting the prison boom's impact within national patterns and across the regions of the state. Third, we trace the ripple effects of prison closure across New York State, based on visits in 2014 to towns across the state that had prisons that have been closed and interviews of town officials. This ethnographic road trip takes us from the abandoned prisons set amidst dairy farms along the Canadian border in the far North, down through the deindustrialized rust belt of central New York, to the bedroom communities, budding art scenes and hipster dives in former prison towns right outside New York. We conclude by pointing toward a reconceptualization of the political economy of both prison towns and, especially, the relationship between poor rural and poor urban areas as they have been reconfigured by over thirty years of mass imprisonment—and the beginnings of significant decarceration.

UNDERSTANDING PRISON PROLIFERATION

As new prisons proliferated nationwide after 1970, battles raged over where to build them and their impact on local communities. Both advocates and critics of prison building assumed that prisons would provide economic and employment benefits to the poor rural communities where the vast majority of prisons were being built. Early studies argued however that prisons impeded economic growth (e.g., Hooks et al. 2004, 48). This conclusion was subsequently called into question (Hooks et al. 2010, 240; King, Mauer, and Huling 2003).

Eason's national study of rural prisons towns from 1970 to 2000s provides a more comprehensive picture and a guidepost for our concern with racial and regional inequalities (Eason 2010; Eason forthcoming; see also Glasmeier and Farrigan 2007). Eason concludes that new prisons do reduce poverty during periods of economic growth and decline, and do replace job losses—but these effects are not long lasting. Contrary to claims regarding the economic benefits of mass incarceration to rural white prison towns, Eason (2010) demonstrates that most prisons in the South were built in rural, black towns with concentrated poverty. The building of prisons across the country in the era of mass incarceration served to link together marginalized and impoverished communities in urban areas, from which most incarcerated people came, and poor rural areas which gained little from prisons. This is a far cry from the images propagated by the media, scholars, and activists of rural people being enriched by mass incarceration. A survey of the prison boom and bust, followed by an extended investigation across the prison towns of New York State, reveals the nature of these links and outcomes—and how they are being transformed in an era of decarceration.

CHARTING THE PRISON BOOM AND IMPACT

New York State was an early center of prison building, trailing only Texas and Florida. Prison building peaked in mid- to late 1980s as Figure 1.1 shows.

Most new prisons were located in rural areas, with state officials often deciding to site clusters of prisons within or near a town.[2] The city of Malone, near the Canadian border, has three prisons, while another seventeen cities have two prisons each. These locations are primarily "upstate," distant from New York City, and located in overwhelmingly conservative political districts: in 2003, 98 percent of prisoners were housed in Republican State Senate districts (Wagner 2004). By the end of the prison boom the average prison incarcerated just over 900 persons at an annual cost of $60,000 per person, and employed almost 400 people.

As prisons were built across the state the character of the towns they were located in significantly shifted.[3] Towns where prisons were built in the 1980s and 1990s had significantly smaller populations and higher percentages of people of color than towns where prisons were built in the 1970s. During the height of the prison-building boom in the 1980s, the average rural town in

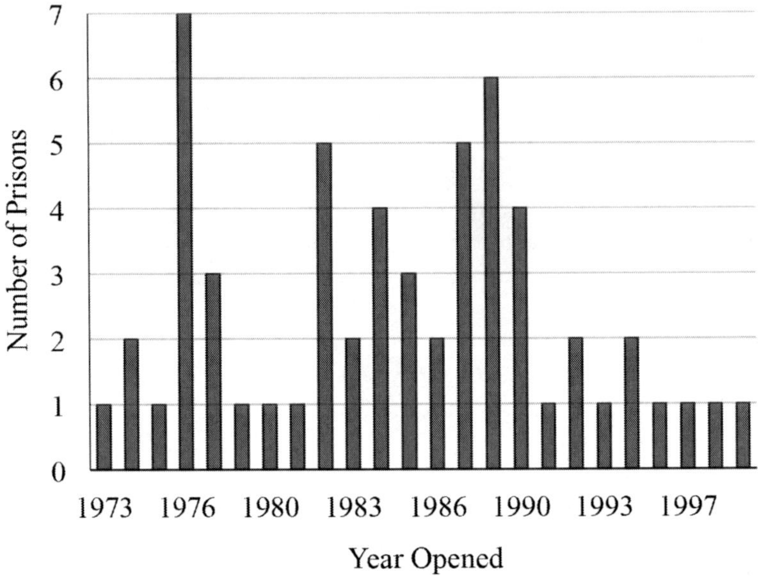

Figure 1.1 New York Prison Boom 1970–2000. *Source*: Data from Eason, n.d.

New York was 97 percent white, while the average town building a prison had twice the percentage of people of color. The new prison towns of the 1980s and 1990s also exhibited greater signs of economic distress, with lower median family incomes and higher rates of unemployment, poverty and joblessness than comparable towns where prisons had not been built. These findings are consistent with national trends, where prisons were overwhelmingly built in areas marked by dense poverty (Eason 2010). While many argue that prisons cause disadvantage (Alexander 2010; Gilmore 2007; Huling 2002; King, Mauer, and Huling 2003), findings suggest that sites for building new prisons in New York State were selected from among the poorest, most disadvantaged, locations.

The economic impact of prisons has varied over time. Towns that adopted prisons by 1980 had, by comparison to towns that did not build a prison, a substantial bump in their median home value, median family income, and percentage of professional managerial workers. However, while white poverty and unemployment rates declined in the new prison towns of the 1980s, black poverty and unemployment increased. If prisons offered some protection to white people from harsh economic winds of the 1970s, this did not extend into the 1980s and 1990s, when home values and employment rates began to decline. By the end of the prison boom, it is clear that prison building was not an economic panacea for struggling towns in New York State.

MAPPING DECARCERATION AND POST-PRISON PLANNING

As the introduction to this volume charts, New York has begun to turn against the wave of prison expansion: since 2009 the doors have been closed on sixteen state prisons. These include prisons in New York City and on its outskirts, and across the rural towns of central, western, and the far north of New York State as Figure 1.2 shows (for further details see appendix A).

Minimum and medium security level prisons were shuttered; not a single maximum security prison was closed. This corresponds to the heavy drop in the number of persons incarcerated for non-violent, primarily drug-related crimes, changes in sentencing laws and new alternatives to incarceration: from 2001 to 2010, the number of inmates housed at maximum security prisons declined by 2 percent, the number of inmates at medium security prisons decreased by 20 percent, and the number at minimum security facilities dropped by 57 percent (Cuomo 2011).

One immediate conclusion is starkly evident: the state prison system as a whole is now more concentrated on maximum and supermax facilities. Why specific prisons were closed and others left open is not easy to determine. The state's oldest, grimmest, and most outdated prisons are still functioning

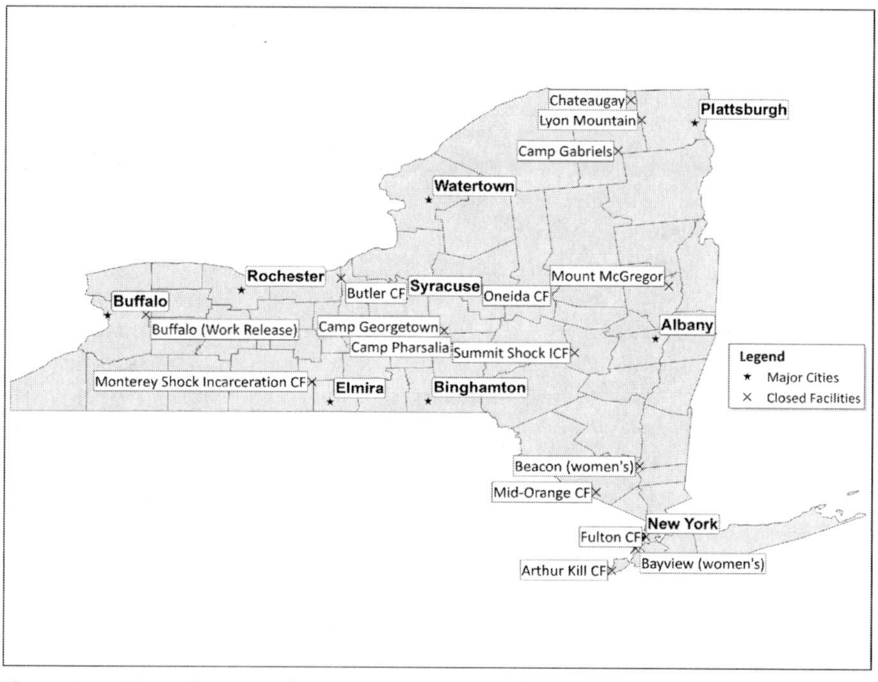

Figure 1.2 Map of New York State. *Source*: Created by Luis R. Gonzalez.

(e.g., Auburn, Attica, Elmira, and Sing Sing, all of which date from the nineteenth or early twentieth century). When interviewed, mayors and town supervisors in prison towns invariably report that they were not consulted over prison closings. This reflects the highly centralized and opaque character of political power and decision-making in New York (Barker 2009, 125–68). The Commissioners of the Department of Correctional Services[4] consistently cited cost savings and efficiencies as criteria, but it is hard to pair these statements with the facilities that were closed. As city officials across the state pointed out, older, remote prisons are more expensive to maintain than the newer prisons that were closed in their towns. A task force was initially charged with compiling a list. This was quickly set aside however when the state legislature delegated the Governor alone to decide which facilities to close. As a result, there is little public evidence on the criteria and process by which specific prisons were selected for termination.

A clue to the puzzle of closing locations is their spatial pattern: many prisons closed by the state were located in or near major urban centers. In New York City alone three prisons closed within its borders, leaving open only Queensboro, a minimum security prison warehousing many charged with parole violations. As a result, a higher proportion of incarcerated people are now located in upstate and rural New York, ever more distant from their families in urban centers.

Small towns without political leverage proved particularly vulnerable. In 2009 the state closed Camp Pharsalia in central New York, a prison for young offenders set in a state forest. At the time the mayor of nearby Norwich (population 7,000) told the press that he expected to lose fifty-nine correctional employees and their families, as well as procurement funds spent at 40 local businesses, and the benefits of incarcerated labor for fifty local organizations and the city. "Where," the mayor asked, "are we going to get another 100,000-plus dollars to hire the additional workers that it would take to replace free prison labor (Richburg 2009)?" Interviewed five years later after the closing of Camp Pharsalia and Camp Georgetown to its north, the mayor detailed a "big loss" in jobs, students from local schools, tax receipts, and local services (Maiurano 2014). Almost all announcements of closures were met by protests from mayors and town supervisors, state representatives, prison employees and their unions—and in one area by prison reform advocates. Newspapers and newscasts stories across the state were filled with accounts of rallies, demonstrations, and delegations to the state capital. Accounts of the prison industrial complex have long maintained that these forces prevented any roll-back of mass incarceration. In New York, however, powerful state unions and local political coalitions have not been able to prevent prison closings.

To be sure, the state assured displaced staff and guards that they would be absorbed in other prisons, and promised local communities assistance in transitioning closed facilities to more productive uses. As part of the Empire State Development (ESD) agency's Economic Transformation Program, closed correctional facilities were eligible for a stake in a fund of $32 million which would be used for renovation purposes, as well as planning possible feasibility or planning studies. Yet a survey of towns that have experienced closures across the state indicate that state redevelopment efforts have returned little to most prison towns, particularly the poorest.

The starkest cases are located in small towns in rural areas, where economic distress is severe, and agricultural alternatives few as the state's leading dairy farming region declines. As recounted by the town supervisor of Chateaugay (population 2,100), a former dairy farmer, it now takes millions of dollars to start a dairy farm, leaving few opportunities for young farmers as small farmers have been driven out by large agro-corporations. The 2014 closing of the Chateaugay prison proved devastating. As the town supervisor noted, "a hundred and eleven jobs in Chateaugay is like 5,000 in a larger city" (Bilow 2014). Just down the road from the closed prison, the sole diner struggles, the school lacks student and parent support, and buildings on the main street collapse for want of repair by absentee landlords. As for the facility itself, a dormitory prison built quickly on land that had "been cheap for a long time," the state, the town supervisor reported, "was removing pretty much everything. It's just going to be an empty shell," which would be "practically given away" (Bilow 2014).

The state had held out a quite different prospect. Six months prior to its closing, the state's development agency, ESD, had issued an adaptive reuse plan for the facility as it had for other prison towns located around the state. Prospective uses included a senior living facility, a call-center, and transforming the facility into a greenhouse and microbrewery with the hopes of creating a more self-sufficient economy for the area (New York State Department of Economic Development 2014b). However, none of these options has been pursued. During our visit in 2014, town officials recounted, moreover, how difficult it was to access the site even for possible investors. In early 2016 the ESD did, finally, commit $4m from the state's prison closing fund—not for the reuse of the prison or to create new jobs, but to save jobs by assisting the upgrading of a local cheese plant.

Meanwhile, ten miles away in Malone (population 14,000), three major prisons remained open—with a large new county jail as well. Malone appeared to be thriving in 2014 despite an assessments ten years earlier that the town would suffer as a result of agreeing to build prisons (Huling 2002, 206; King, Mauer, and Huling 2003, 5, 15). Like many towns across the state, in the twentieth century Malone had been a regional manufacturing and transport hub, with foundries, a woolen factory, railroad workshops and a state police headquarters. These all began to wither away after World War II. Successful bids for two large, medium security prisons in the late 1980s, followed by a supermax in 1998, provided the basis for countering deindustrialization. The state, in short, "took away the cops [state police] and gave us the robbers" (Maneely 2014). The town supervisor himself came to his position from this shift to mass incarceration, having retired from the Department of Corrections in the late 1990s as a deputy superintendent. Today the town boasts a Walmart Supercenter, Holiday Inn, Red Roof Inn, 36 hole golf course, ski center, and bustling downtown.

The rural southern shore of Lake Ontario, 165 miles to the southwest, provides a clear contrast. The Butler prison, like Chateaugay's, was a late addition to the state's stock of prisons in the northern rural reaches of the state, opening in 1989 as a shock (military-style, "boot camp") facility and expanding to house both minimum and medium security wings. It too closed in late 2014 (New York State Department of Economic Development 2014a). There were multiple community reuse proposals. The biggest obstacle was funding—and market demand. The proposals included institutional uses such as a health services facility for veterans, a job training facility, or a rehabilitation center. Commercial uses included a campus for high-tech companies and an office park. The most immediate replacement proposal was to turn the state prison into a county jail, a common proposal in many towns (New York State Department of Economic Development 2014a). As of late 2015, the facility remains empty.

Heading sixty-five miles south to a state forest in central New York one finds the oldest of the four facilities closed in 2014, Monterey Shock, which had 124 full-time employees in late 2013. Community proposals included keeping the facility as a correctional facility, using the site for game land, or creating a tourist destination (New York. Department of Economic Development 2015). In October 2014 it was announced that the Schuyler County Partnership for Economic Development and the Schuyler County Planning Department were working with students from Cornell University to develop possible reuse plans for the facility. No updates have come from any of the participating organizations as of spring 2015.

Much the same story can be told as one moves downstate to the Mount McGregor prison on a hilltop overlooking the town of Wilton, located 120 miles south of Chateaugay, 170 miles north of New York City, and near Saratoga Springs, an affluent resort destination for over a century. Mount McGregor became a luxurious resort in the late nineteenth century, served by a railroad line that brought up wealthy residents of New York City to the cooler mountain air; it was there that President Ulysses S. Grant spent his last six weeks in a cottage, completing his memoirs before he died in 1885. In 1913 it became a private TB sanitarium, only later to become a state health facility and in 1960 a state school for mentally challenged students.

In 1976 it was taken over by the New York State Department of Corrections and turned into a minimum-security camp, with an additional medium-security section added later. In 2009 the camp portion of the facility closed, and in 2014 the medium-security section shut its doors. Since the Grant Cottage State Historic Site sits on the grounds of the prison, several community proposals included transforming the area into a park for tourists. Other proposals included an adult care facility, a casino, or transferring at least part of the facility's 1,200 acres to the adjoining Moreau Lake State Park for recreational, educational, and wildlife preservation. As of late 2015, 750 acres were being converted to a state park; the remaining 350 acres and the prison's 100 buildings remain abandoned.

The failure to implement reuse proposals points to the continuing lack of private or public commitment or investment. With little investment flowing to the upstate economy, civilians are left to fend for themselves and their families through service jobs. This situation has been made worse as government employment has steadily declined in recent years.[5] And when rural former prison sites do sell, they sell at low prices. As of 2015, only two of the facilities located upstate, Camp Georgetown and Summit Shock, have been sold—but remain undeveloped and unused.

DECARCERATION SUCCESS STORIES?

As one approaches New York City these calculations and conclusions begin to change radically. One key difference is apparent immediately: while mayors in the northern and central regions of the state agonized and battled vociferously to retain prisons, this was not the case as one moved nearer to New York City. Local resignation and even acceptance of prison closings cannot be explained by political decision-making alone. Here the political economy of areas closely tied to New York City sheds considerable light.

Certainly the extraordinary value of some New York City prison properties, located in gentrifying neighborhoods or towns, provided the state with an incentive to close and sell them. An additional and substantial clue was provided early one morning in Moreau, New York, as an author went to a corner deli for breakfast, before a meeting with the mayor and a visit to the abandoned Mt. McGregor prison complex. Parked outside at 6:30 am were large pickup trucks, while inside construction workers were ordering the "heart attack special" (a massive egg, bacon, sausage, and cheese breakfast sandwich). As a local hotel owner later explained, the city and county were booming due to a $5 billion computer chip factory being constructed nearby—solicited originally with over $1.4 billion in state tax credits and a direct $635 million cash grant (Thomas 2011, 90; the plant became a $10 billion project with new expansions). Local hotels in surrounding counties were full of the 5,000 workers involved, the town budget was in surplus, and tourism was an additional mainstay of the local economy (Johnson 2014). In this climate the closure of even a large prison complex hardly worried town officials.

Much the same story could be told of Beacon, New York. In the early nineteenth century, Beacon, situated on the Hudson River, became a manufacturing center producing cotton cloth and rugs. Late in the century it was renowned as the "hat capital" of the country (Murphy 1998, 35–46). A century later, like so many towns upstate, only the empty shells of multi-story, brick factories remain. Beacon, however, is situated a little over an hour away from New York City by commuter train. The financial boom and the gentrification of New York have made Beacon a "bedroom" community: a major art center has opened, new residents are commuting to jobs in New York City, and a new Sushi restaurant, Italian trattoria, and olive oil bar attest to the afterglow effect of Wall Street excess.

These developments made the mayor, "one of the luckiest, because we're just the right distance from New York City; we have the train station right here." On weekends, the town's main street is often flooded, the mayor went on, by "flocks of younger people from New York City" and "day trippers [who] come up from New York City starting on Thursday, spending money, and hanging out at new venues and restaurants" (Casale 2014). The closure of a small women's prison has thus imposed little hardship. The future of the town clearly lies elsewhere, south along the railway line. Indeed, a major worry of many residents was that wealthy newcomers would become so numerous that they would crowd out the historic working and middle classes of the city. In this scenario, those who had grown up in the city for generations would "no longer be able to afford" to live in the city (Casale 2014).

For the town of Warwick (population 32,000), faced with the closure of the large Mid-Orange prison in 2011, proximity to New York City (40 miles away) and a sophisticated local initiative played a key role in determining an unusual outcome: a local development consortium (LDC) was quickly formed and pushed hard to convince the state to sell to the LDC the prison's buildings and 150 acres of the site's 738 acres (Walsh 2014). The cost was $3.5 million, a sum far beyond the means of poor rural communities. The site was quickly rezoned, and by 2014 Trans Tech, a private company producing small electric buses, was leasing two large warehouses for its operations (Sweeten 2015). In 2015 a recreational building was sold to a sports training company, and in early 2016 it was announced that a Chinese consortium was closing a $1.7 million deal to turn the main prison site into a hotel and spa complex. The lesson for other ex-prison towns, the town supervisor responded, was "don't wait for the state to come in and do something good." (Sweeten 2015).

The closing of three of the four prisons within New York City's boundaries underscores the benefits of proximity to New York City. Community reactions were not at all like those upstate, with the most striking difference the way prison reform advocates opposed the closing of these prisons close to New York City. They argued that closing facilities, especially women's facilities, was counter to the interests of the incarcerated, their families who wanted to visit, and their communities (Correctional Association 2013). In other cases in New York City, people opposed opening new facilities. New York City residents protested the opening of a federal prison near JFK airport and new youth detention centers in Staten Island and Queens (CBS News 2013; Gronda 2015). The 2001 closing of the Arthur Kill prison in Staten Island was also welcomed locally, and it was eventually sold for $7 million to a movie production studio firm.

The outcome for the Fulton prison in the Bronx, the poorest borough with much lower land values, was markedly different. Here a reuse proposal for a reentry services facility came to fruition in early 2015. It was certainly needed: there are approximately 15,000 residents of the borough on parole and probation (Rivera 2013). This was not, however, a program to be run by state or city social service agencies, but marked rather carceral devolution: a private nonprofit, the Osborne Association, was given a $6 million state grant to rehab the facility into a venue for job training, temporary housing, and other social services (King 2013). The transition is a slow one however: when the authors visited in April 2015, a soundstage crew was using the empty building for a film shoot.

A similar plan awaits the Bayview Correctional Facility in Manhattan, a former YMCA which had become a medium-security prison for women. Overlooking the Hudson and surrounded now by high-end art galleries and luxury condo buildings, Bayview was evacuated in October 2012 after Hurricane Sandy flooded part of the building. Unlike upstate facilities, its reuse by the private sector was delayed due to the state's ruling out its most profitable replacement as a luxury housing development. In late 2015 it was announced that a developer and a Warren Buffet family nonprofit would convert the Art Deco building into offices, an art gallery, and a wellness center operated by nonprofit organizations serving women.

DECARCERATION, DEVOLUTION, AND JUSTICE DISINVESTMENT

Political power exercised at the level of the Governor's office has been a key factor in determining which prisons close. The fate of prisons towns is now, in ways unimaginable in earlier decades, increasingly dependent upon newfound support for the private sector and nongovernmental agencies. And these take place in turn against the remarkable transformations of the political economy of New York in recent decades.

Accounts of mass incarceration emphasize the rise of bipartisan criminal justice policies in the 1970s and 1980s. At the same time as prisons were being built, factories and firms were closing their doors all across the state, leaving behind remnants of small and once-great manufacturing firms, from Kodak in Rochester, to IBM in Endicott, to Corning Glass in Corning, to the empty Studebaker automotive plant that still towers over West Harlem. Competition and concentration in the agricultural sector, particularly in the dairy industry, undermined the state's small-scale farming sector. Faced with these long-term trends, both Republican and Democratic governors placed prisons during the prison boom years in disadvantaged, poor, and largely white rural sections of the state.

The movement to decarcerate over the last fifteen years takes place, however, amidst significant shifts in the long-term, regional patterns of economic opportunity, wealth, and political power. On the one hand, the Great Recession of 2008 accelerated the employment difficulties faced by people living in upstate communities: an additional 170,000 manufacturing jobs alone disappeared between 2000 and 2010 (Abel 2014), while dairy farming, the state's primary agricultural sector (and the nation's third largest) employing 20,000 people, continued to shrink steadily (New York State Office of the State Comptroller 2010).

On the other hand, new wealth has concentrated in New York City. Economically, New York State's fortunes now derive, far more than any other state, from the rise of speculative financial capital and the cultural attractions of New York City for the country's elite, international tourists, and real estate developers. This has served to polarize incomes and inequality between upstate and downstate communities, as well as within the parts of New York city that are gentrifying; a full 45 percent of New York City's population remains below or near the poverty line (New York City Office of the Mayor 2014). In a very real sense both poor upstate communities and poor downstate communities have been steadily and impoverished alike in the decarceration era.

Nowhere are these trends more evident than in the fate of prison towns. A few fortunate towns within the orbit of New York City have seen prisons replaced to some degree by the new wealth generated by the rise of the financial, real estate, and tourist sectors. The state's use of economic development funds to support private, high-tech industries, and in some cases private and public educational institutions, has supported some commuter towns as well by shifting state funds and employment to the private sector. The future of the old manufacturing and agricultural towns of upstate New York is much bleaker: they have no place in these new stories of government and financial sector largesse. By concentrating prisons in ever yet poorer areas marked by the forces of economic underdevelopment, decarceration promises to accelerate inequality within and across the state.

This conclusion is enhanced by the findings of other chapters in two critical areas. One, closing prisons has meant that ever-larger numbers of formerly incarcerated persons are being sent to urban neighborhoods marked by extreme poverty and unemployment. Prison towns and urban ghettos thus both face a future of further underdevelopment: isolated prison towns close down and communities fall into greater distress, while incarcerated men and women return to tightly policed and supervised neighborhoods that pose a maze of obstacles to finding a job, a home, and family life.

Decarceration is also increasingly marked by the replacement of past decades' "carceral Keynesianism," or the pump-priming of state economies by investments in prisons (Gilmore 2007), with the diversion of state funds to direct and indirect subsidies to the private sector. These instances range, as we have seen above, from state assistance to Chateaugay's faltering cheese plant in the far North, through subsidies to high-tech firms in western and central New York, to turning over prison spaces to film production firms and nonprofits in and around New York City. This redirection of state funds and employment is further entrenched by the use of nonprofit agencies to perform many criminal justice functions previously contained within prison walls. These developments extend devolution as charted in other chapters: the turning over of state criminal justice supervision to non-state agencies (nonprofit and profit social agencies, reentry service providers, community-based organizations, etc.). Disinvestment in rural communities is matched, in short, by state disinvestment in the dirty tasks of the criminal justice process itself. Recuperation from decades of mass incarceration under these conditions slips ever farther away.

These trends take us far away from the expectation of what closing prisons might mean for the formerly incarcerated and their segregated towns and neighborhoods. Based on the evidence before us, decarceration as rolled out by the state is making an unexpected contribution to the growing gap between the rich and poor across the state.

APPENDIX A

Table 1.1 Prison Closings 2009–2014[6]

Region/Prison	Level	Head Count (2010)	Closing Date	Town (2010 population 1,000s)
New York City				
Arthur Kill	Medium	918	December 2011	Staten Island (470)
Bayview	Medium	165	October 2012	Manhattan (1,588)
Fulton	Minimum	127	October 2011	Bronx (1,388)
Far North				
Camp Gabriels	Minimum	189 (2009)	July 2009	Brighton (36)
Chateaugay	Medium	201	July 2014	Chateaugay (2)
Lyon Mountain	Minimum	109	January 2011	Dannemora (5)
Hudson Valley				
Beacon	Minimum	168	September 2013	Beacon (16)
Mid-Orange	Medium	655	August 2011	Warwick (32)
Western NY				
Buffalo	Minimum	121	2012	Alden (11)
Butler	Medium	70	July 2014	Red Creek (0.5)
Monterey Shock	Minimum	141	July 2014	Orange (1.7)
Central NY				
Camp Georgetown	Minimum	148	October 2011	Georgetown (1)
Camp Pharsalia	Minimum	106 (2009)	January 2009	Pharsalia (0.6)
Mt. McGregor	Medium	462	July 2014	Wilton (16)
Oneida	Medium	469	October 2011	Rome (34)
Summit Shock	Minimum	134	July 2011	Summit (1)

Sources: The New York State Department of Corrections and Community Supervision, "Facility Listing," 2009, 2014, http://www.doccs.ny.gov/faclist.html; The New York State Department of Corrections and Community Supervision, "2011 Prison Closures," http://www.doccs.ny.gov/FactSheets/PrisonClosure2011.html, accessed March 4, 2015; Prisoners of the Census, "Correctional Facility Locator 2010," 2011, 2014, http://www.prisonersofthecensus.org/locator2010/states/starts-with-New%20York/ and "Census 2000 Correctional Facility Locator," 2002, 2014, http://www.prisonersofthecensus.org/locator/; and local news reports (used in the discussion of prison closings).[7]

NOTES

1. The authors wish to gratefully acknowledge the assistance of Brenda Freeman in transcribing interview materials, and the guidance and critical comments of our research group, including particularly Josh Price as well as Chungse Jung, Brendan McQuade, Andrew Pragacz, and Kevin Revier.

2. Not every prison was newly constructed; in a number of cases prisons were conversions of health or reformatory institutions (e.g., among those recently closed, the Arthur Kill, Fulton, and Bayview [all in New York City], and the Mid-Orange and Mt. McGregor prisons [see Table 1.1]).

3. The findings in the next two paragraphs are drawn from a national dataset developed by the author (Eason n.d.).

4. In 2011, the New York State Department of Correctional Services (DOCS) and the Division of Parole (DOP) were merged under the new name of the Department of Corrections and Community Supervision (DOCCS).

5. The state was, before 2009, the second largest employer and particularly important in upstate and rural areas. From 2009 through 2014, the government sector shrank by 6 percent, losing 87,000 jobs (New York State Office of the State Comptroller 2015, 5–6).

6. The Department of Corrections and Community Services divides its prisons into nine administrative "Hubs," which do not easily match other common definitions of regions for the purposes of economic development, tourism, or political and civic boundaries; there is no accepted official state or popular definition of the state's regions. We have regrouped these nine into fewer, more common regions: Far North (Watertown and Clinton Hubs), Western (Wende and Elmira Hubs), Central (Oneida and Great Meadow Hub), Hudson Valley (Sullivan and Green Haven Hub) and New York City (New York City Hub). See New York State Department of Correctional and Community Supervision (2013) for current state definitions.

7. Including: *Auburn Citizen*, "What Does the Future Hold for Now-Closed Butler Correctional Facility in Wayne County?" August 3, 2014, http://auburnpub.com/blogs/eye_on_ny/what-does-the-future-hold-for-now-closed-butler-correctional/article_2d633966-1980-11e4-a6c2-001a4bcf887a.html, accessed March 3, 2015; The *Wall Street Journal*, "Former Prison in Manhattan Could Be Tough Sell," January 28, 2014, http://www.wsj.com/articles/SB10001424052702304691904579348883798778354, accessed March 4, 2015; *Poughkeepsie Journal*, "State: How Best to Spend $6 Million to Soften Blow of Beacon Prison Closure," January 19, 2014, http://www.poughkeepsiejournal.com/article/20140119/NEWS01/301190062/State-How-best-spend-6-million-soften-blow-Beacon-prison-closure, accessed March 4, 2015; *Time Warner Cable News*, "Monterey Shock Incarceration Correctional Facility Closes Its Doors," July 28, 2014, http://www.twcnews.com/archives/nys/central-ny/2014/07/28/monterey-shock-incarceration-correctional-facility-closes-its-doors-NY_756409.old.html, accessed March 4, 2015; *New York Daily News*, "Shuttered Bronx Prison to Be Used as Job-Training and Reentry Center for the Formerly Incarcerated," January 31, 2013, http://www.nydailynews.com/new-york/bronx/gov-cuomo-budget-plans-renovate-old-jail-curb-recidivism-article-1.1250698, accessed March 4, 2015; *The Times Union*, "Empty Upstate Prison is Sold," May 9, 2013, http://www.timesunion.com/local/article/Empty-upstate-prison-is-sold-4504271.php, accessed March 4, 2015; *The Daily Star*, "Former Prison in Schoharie is Up for Auction" August 19, 2014, http://www.thedailystar.com/news/local_news/article_53f8f796-96da-5d5a-9a95-bdc167e8a3c2.html, accessed March 4, 2015; *CBS New York*, "Staten Island, Bronx Prisons Among Those Now Closed In New York," January 3, 2012, http://newyork.cbslocal.com/2012/01/03/staten-island-bronx-prisons-among-those-now-closed-in-new-york/, accessed March 4, 2015; *New York Times*, "New York Has Some Prisons to Sell You," May 27, 2013, http://www.nytimes.com/2012/05/28/nyregion/closed-new-york-prisons-prove-hard-to-sell.html?pagewanted=all&_r=0, accessed March 4, 2015; *The Times Herald*, "Warwick Taking on Former Mid-Orange Correctional Facility," July 27, 2013, http://www.recordonline.com/article/20130727/News/307270329, accessed March 4, 2015; *WPTZ, News Channel 5*, "Chateaugay Community Holds Rally to Keep Prison Open," October 6, 2013, http://www.wptz.com/news/vermont-new-york/plattsburgh/chateaugay-community-holds-rally-to-keep-prison-open/22296376,

accessed March 4, 2015; *The Times Union*, "Prison Set to Close, But Not Quietly," July 25, 2014, http://www.timesunion.com/local/article/Prison-set-to-close-but-not-quietly-5648057.php, accessed March 4, 2015; *Press-Republican*, "Camp Gabriels to Close July 1," April 15, 2009, http://www.pressrepublican.com/news/local_news/article_a111957b-9310-5a8f-b0e9-c3ce6bba7319.html, accessed March 4, 2015; *WBNG-TV*, "Camp Pharsalia Closing," July 22, 2010, http://www.wbng.com/closings/44085767.html, accessed March 4, 2015; Fusion, "Inside the Abandoned New York Prison That's Been Taken Over By Activists," November 9, 2015, http://fusion.net/story/229163/inside-bayview-abandoned-new-york-prison/, accessed March 15, 2016; *timesunion*, "Sale of Adirondack Prison Hits Snag: It's in the Forest Preserve," June 3, 2015, http://www.timesunion.com/news/article/Sale-of-Adirondack-prison-hits-snag-It-s-in-the-6305690.php, accessed March 6, 2016; The Warwick Advertiser, "Transfer of 36 Acres at the Former Prison Completed," January 7, 2015, http://www.warwickadvertiser.com/apps/pbcs.dll/article?AID=/20150107/NEWS01/150109970/Transfer-of-36-acres-at-the-former-prison-completed, accessed March 8, 2016; *Times Herald-Record*, December 28, 2015, http://www.recordonline.com/article/20151228/NEWS/151229581, accessed March 4, 2016; Syracuse.com, "Former NY Prison Could Become Yoga Retreat Center, New Owner Says," June 24, 2015, http://www.syracuse.com/state/index.ssf/2015/06/former_ny_prison_could_become_yoga_retreat_center_new_owner_says.html, accessed March 16, 2016; *Times Journal*, "Fulton junk yard decision put on hold," http://www.timesjournalonline.com/details.asp?id=96953, accessed March 18, 2016.

REFERENCES

Abel, Jaison R. 2014. "Economic Conditions in Upstate New York." New York: Federal Reserve Bank of New York. Upstate New York Regional Advisory Council Meeting. http://www.newyorkfed.org/aboutthefed/pdf/UNYRAB_June%203_AgendaandPresentations.pdf. Accessed March 30, 2015.

Alexander, Michelle. 2010. *The New Jim Crow: Mass Incarceration in the Age of Colorblindness*. New York: New Press.

Barker, Vanessa. 2009. *The Politics of Imprisonment: How the Democratic Process Shapes the Way America Punishes Offenders*. Studies in Crime and Public Policy. Oxford; New York: Oxford University Press.

Bilow, Don. 2014 Interview by William G. Martin.

Casale, Randy. 2014 Interview by William G. Martin.

CBS News. 2013. "Staten Island Residents to Protest Proposed Juvenile Detention Facility." CBS New York, October 23. http://newyork.cbslocal.com/2013/10/23/staten-island-residents-to-protest-proposed-juvenile-detention-facility/. Accessed April 28, 2015.

Correctional Association. 2013. "Bayview and Beacon Closures May Mean Lost Opportunities for Women in Prison." January 30. http://www.correctionalassociation.org/press/nys-prison-closures-may-mean-lost-opportunities-for-women. Accessed March 21, 2015.

Cuomo, Governor Andrew M. 2011. "Governor Cuomo Announces Closure of Seven State Prison Facilities." Governor's Press Office. https://www.governor.ny.gov/press/06302011ClosureOfSevenStatePrisonFacilities. Accessed October 3, 2014.

Eason, John. 2010. "Mapping Prison Proliferation: Region, Rurality, Race and Disadvantage in Prison Placement." *Social Science Research* 39 (6): 1015–28. doi:10.1016/j.ssresearch.2010.03.001.

———. Forthcoming 2017. *Big House on the Prairie: Rise of the Rural Ghetto & Prison Proliferation*. Chicago: University of Chicago Press.

———. n.d. Prison Proliferation Project database. Unpublished.

Foucault, Michel. 1977. *Discipline and Punish: The Birth of the Prison*. 1st American ed. New York: Pantheon Books.

Gilmore, Ruth Wilson. 2007. *Golden Gulag: Prisons, Surplus, Crisis, and Opposition in Globalizing California*. Berkeley: University of California Press.

Glasmeier, Amy K., and Tracey Farrigan. 2007. "The Economic Impacts of the Prison Development Boom on Persistently Poor Rural Places." *International Regional Science Review* 30 (3): 274–99. doi:10.1177/0160017607301608.

Gronda, Luis. 2015. "Residents Against Youth Home Protest At CB9." *Queens Tribune*, February 15. http://queenstribune.com/residents-against-youth-home-protest-at-cb9/. Accessed April 15, 2015.

Hooks, Gregory, Clayton Mosher, Shaun Genter, Thomas Rotolo, and Linda Lobao. 2010. "Revisiting the Impact of Prison Building on Job Growth: Education, Incarceration, and County-Level Employment, 1976–2004." *Social Science Quarterly* 91 (1): 228–44. doi:10.1111/j.1540-6237.2010.00690.x.

Hooks, Gregory, Clayton Mosher, Thomas Rotolo, and Linda Lobao. 2004. "The Prison Industry: Carceral Expansion and Employment in U.S. Counties, 1969–1994." *Social Science Quarterly* 85 (1): 37–57. doi:10.1111/j.0038-4941.2004.08501004.x.

Huling, Tracy. 2002. "Building a Prison Economy in Rural America." In *Invisible Punishment: The Collateral Consequences of Mass Imprisonment*, edited by Marc Mauer and Meda Chesney-Lind, 197–213. New York: The New Press.

Johnson, Town Supervisor Arthur. 2014 Interview by William G. Martin.

King, David H. 2013. "Can Empty Prisons Be Repurposed to Help Ex-Cons Reintegrate Into Society?" April 23. http://www.gothamgazette.com/index.php/public-safety/4228-can-empty-prisons-be-repurposed-to-help-ex-cons-reintegrate-into-society. Accessed March 20, 2015.

King, Ryan S., Marc Mauer, and Tracy Huling. 2003. "Big Prisons, Small Towns: Prison Economics in Rural America." The Sentencing Project. http://sentencingproject.org/doc/inc_bigprisons.pdf. Accessed April 12, 2015.

Maiurano, Mayor Joseph. 2014 Interview by William G. Martin.

Maneely, Howard F. 2014 Interview by William Martin.

Murphy, Robert J. 1998. *Historic Beacon. Images of America*. Charleston, SC: Arcadia.

New York City. Office of the Mayor. 2014. "The CEO Poverty Measure, 2005–2012. An Annual Report from the Office of the Mayor." New York. http://www.nycppf.org/html/ceo/downloads/pdf/ceo_poverty_measure_2005_2013.pdf. Accessed April 28, 2015.

New York. Department of Economic Development. 2015. "Report for the Adaptive Re-Use of Monterey Shock Incarceration Correctional Facility." http://esd.ny.gov/Resources/Properties/1-26-2014_MontereyShock.pdf. Accessed March 19.

New York State Department of Corrections and Community Supervision. 2013. "New York State Department of Corrections and Community Supervision Facilities and Regional Map." Albany, NY. http://www.doccs.ny.gov/facilitymapcolor.pdf. Accessed October 4, 2014.

New York State Department of Economic Development. 2014a. "Report for the Adaptive Re-Use of Butler Correctional Facility." http://esd.ny.gov/Resources/Properties/1-26-2014_ButlerCF.pdf. Accessed March 19, 2015.

———. 2014b. "Report for the Adaptive Re-Use of Chateaugay Correctional Facility." http://esd.ny.gov/Resources/Properties/1-26-2014_ChateaugayCF.pdf. Accessed March 19, 2015.

New York State Office of the State Comptroller. 2010. "New York's Dairy Industry in Crisis." https://www.osc.state.ny.us/localgov/pubs/research/snapshot/0310snapshot.pdf. Accessed March 30, 2015.

———. 2015. "New York State Employment Trends." Albany, NY: New York State. www.osc.state.ny.us/reports/economic/employment_trends_nys_2015.pdf. Accessed March 14, 2016.

Richburg, Keith B. 2009. "Plan for Prison Closures Stirs Fears." *Washington Post*, March 22. http://www.washingtonpost.com/wp-dyn/content/article/2009/03/22/AR2009032200012.html. Accessed March 5, 2015.

Rivera, State Senator Gustavo. 2013. "Senator Rivera Speaks on the Transfer of the Fulton Correctional Facility in the Bronx." March 27. http://www.nysenate.gov/press-release/senator-rivera-speaks-transfer-fulton-correctional-facility-bronx. Accessed March 18, 2015.

Schlosser, Eric. 1998. "The Prison Industrial Complex." *The Atlantic Monthly* 282 (6): 51–77.

Sweeten, Michael. 2015 Interview by William G Martin.

Thomas, Kenneth P. 2011. *Investment Incentives and the Global Competition for Capital*. New York: Palgrave Macmillan.

Wagner, Peter. 2004. "Temporary Populations Change the Political Face of New York; 98% of NY's Prison Cells Are in Republican Senate Districts." August 30. http://www.prisonersofthecensus.org/news/2004/08/30/temporary-populations/. Accessed October 1, 2014.

Walsh, James. 2014. "Warwick, Orange County See Future Profit in Former Mid-Orange Correctional Facility." *Times-Herald Record*, August 30. http://www.recordonline.com/article/20140830/News/140829621. Accessed March 20, 2015.

Chapter 2

Media and the New War on Drugs

Governing through Meth

Kevin Revier, Chungse Jung, and William G. Martin

Speaking at a town-hall meeting in Kingston, Jamaica in 2015, President Barack Obama declared the war on drugs an unproductive exercise that had torn apart families and led to more crime.[1] Two years earlier, Attorney-General Eric Holder called for reform of some of the harshest sentencing laws. Congress passed the Fair Sentencing Act of 2010 and several states have established drug courts, community-based alternatives to prison, and less draconian sentencing laws (Greene et al. 2010; Ahrens 2010). In New York State, the legislature rolled back a three strikes law and fifteen-year mandatory minimum sentences that were part of the 1973 Rockefeller Drug Laws (Mancuso 2010; Parsons et al. 2015). The number of imprisoned drug offenders in New York State subsequently dropped from 24,085 in 1996 to 7,053 in 2012 (New York State Department of Corrections and Community Supervision 2013). Drug reform, prison closings, and the decline in prison populations signify important movement away from the decades-long mass incarceration era.

Let's contrast these changes with news coverage of the 2015 election race for a new district attorney in Broome County, in Central New York. Republican Steve Cornwell beat the incumbent in a tightly fought race in which the war on drugs featured prominently. According to the Binghamton *Press & Sun-Bulletin*, Cornwell said in his acceptance speech, "Our focus will be on the heroin and drug epidemic." The reporter went on to observe,

> The county's struggle with heroin and opiate addiction, which has taken an increasing toll in lives and law enforcement resources over the past three years, was a key topic for both candidates. Through the campaign, Cornwell accused the district attorney's office of lapses in prosecution and an outdated mindset ill-equipped to deal with the opiate problem.[2]

How do we reconcile these two snapshots—in one, a national call for a rethinking of the war on drugs along with a steep decline in incarceration for drug crimes, and the other with an emphasis on drug crime as an emergent problem in an upstate community? Indeed, the latter example seems to follow a style of drug scare politics and reporting that runs counter to recent efforts in decriminalization and reform. It follows a long tradition of drug scares which have primarily served to criminalize "outsider" groups (Reinarman and Levine 1989; Taylor 2008). From the anti-Chinese opium scare and the 1914 Harrison Narcotics Act, to the anti-Mexican marijuana scare and the 1937 Marihuana Tax Act, and through to the most recent anti-black and anti-Latina/o crack scare and harsh sentencing laws, drug scares "have been a recurring feature of U.S. society for 200 years" (Reinarman 1994, 92; Reinarman and Levine 1989). The war on drugs operated as a war on people of color and a contributing factor to the building of the carceral state (Mauer 2006; Wacquant 2009; Alexander 2010).

The radical decline in the number of people incarcerated for drug crimes in New York raises the question of whether crime and drug scares still matter. Has media coverage of crime and drugs changed as both crime rates *and* incarceration rates have fallen? Has decarceration preceded or been accompanied by shifts in media coverage on crime? To explore these questions, we track crime and drug coverage in nineteen New York State newspapers, starting with a comparison of crime rates and the number of crime articles published over the last ten years. We find an anomalous pattern for meth (methamphetamine) reporting, which matches the wide national coverage of the drug in recent years. We then conduct a content analysis of meth articles in a single newspaper to gain insight on the relationship between meth reporting, policing, and decarceration.

We arrive at three conclusions. First, despite a drop in crime overall and a drop in drug stories in the major urban areas, coverage of crime and drugs has *increased* in rural areas and smaller cities and towns. Second, an analysis of media content reveals that meth reporting stigmatizes and criminalizes rural spaces, producing images of rural degradation and decay, while imagining the "rural" as a space of insecurity in need of state-led intervention (Banks 2005; Linnemann 2013). Third, reporters writing about meth legitimize and at times participate in surveillance and policing across upstate New York. They facilitate interagency collaboration across the public/private divide and the use of new technologies for intelligence-led policing (Feeley and Simon 1992; see chapter 3 by McQuade).

Our analysis demonstrates that meth reporting does not support efforts towards the reform of drug laws passed during the period of mass incarceration nor does it represent a mere expansion of the carceral state to rural areas. Rather, the meth scare aids in the devolution of the carceral state.

This supports the movement of carceral authority to local actors, while facilitating social control during decarceration (Miller 2014, 308).

GOVERNING STATEWIDE THROUGH CRIME AND DRUGS

The meth scare is a product of a larger process of "governing through crime," a project that began with Nixon's presidency and the Safe Street Act of 1968 and accelerated with mass incarceration through the end of the last century (Simon 2007). Its key elements comprise the use of crime as a strategic policy issue, framing social problems or issues as a question of criminality to justify intervention, and the institutional adoption of crime discourse in the family, school, and workplace. Although crime coverage and actual crime rates bear little relation, it has played an essential role in producing a culture of fear and legitimizing efforts to build the incarcerating state (Simon 2007, 5; Beckett and Sasson 2003).

Before focusing directly on the meth scare, in order to examine the general relationship between drug and crime reporting and decarceration we created a dataset recording the frequency and visibility of popular crime-related and drug-related stories for nineteen newspapers in New York State (for the method and the list of newspapers, see appendix A). Since one cannot presume that media coverage is stable across time or urban and rural regions (Banks 2005; Weidner 2009), we created separate datasets for two New York City newspapers and seventeen regional newspapers across the state. The latter were further segmented into five newspapers from larger metropolitan areas in upstate New York (Albany, Buffalo, Rochester, and Syracuse) and twelve newspapers from smaller upstate cities and towns (Auburn, Batavia, Binghamton, Canandaigua, Corning, Elmira, Hornell, Hudson, Ithaca, Plattsburgh, Utica, and Watertown).

The findings are striking. As Figure 2.1 shows, the number of headlines related to *crime* in New York City newspapers fell between 2003 and 2014.

Larger metropolitan areas in upstate New York have seen a dramatic decline in crime coverage. A strong counterpoint is offered however by media visibility and frequency in the smaller cities, towns, and rural areas of upstate New York. In these areas crime coverage steadily *increased* between 2003 and 2011, and remains high as of 2014. The number of major index crimes (murder, rape, robbery, and aggravated assault; and property crimes of burglary, larceny, and motor vehicle theft)[3] has fallen steadily since 1990 in all these regions as Figure 2.2 shows.

Media panics produce more coverage of actual crime events (see Williams and Dickinson 1993). Did changes in newspaper coverage, as revealed by Figure 2.1, relate at all to changes in crime rates in different regions?

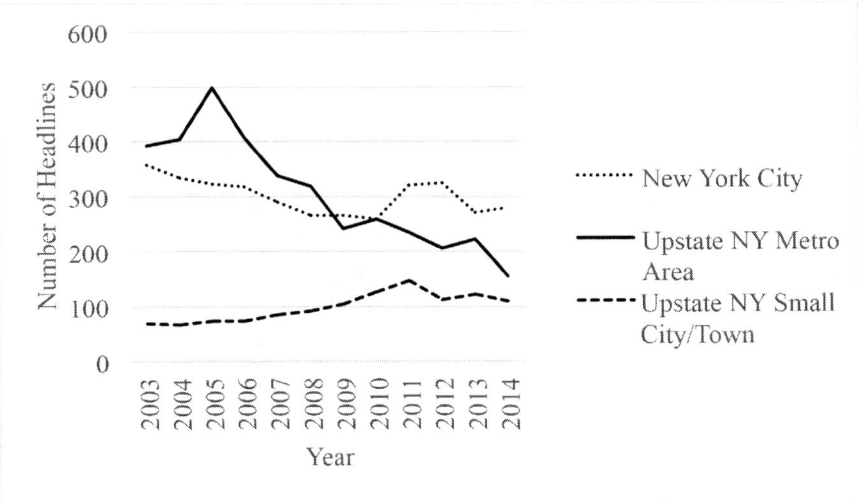

Figure 2.1 Average Number of Crime Headlines, 2003–2014. *Source*: Author's compilation; see appendix A for sources and details.

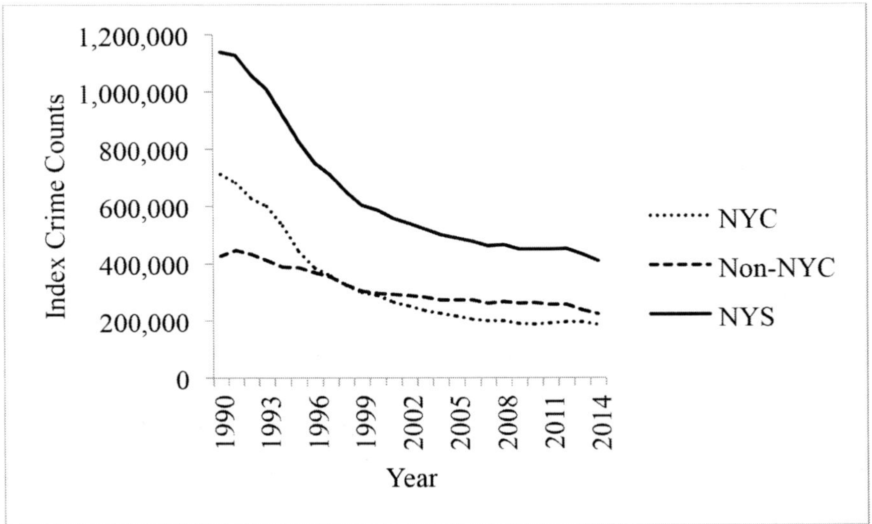

Figure 2.2 New York State Index Crime Counts, 1990–2014. *Source*: Data from New York State Division of Criminal Justice Services (2015).

To explore this we created a dataset to evaluate newspapers' coverage rates of crime beyond what could be justified by actual crime rates. Figure 2.3 shows the average number of *crime* headlines per one hundred index crime counts by different regions (for details see appendix A).

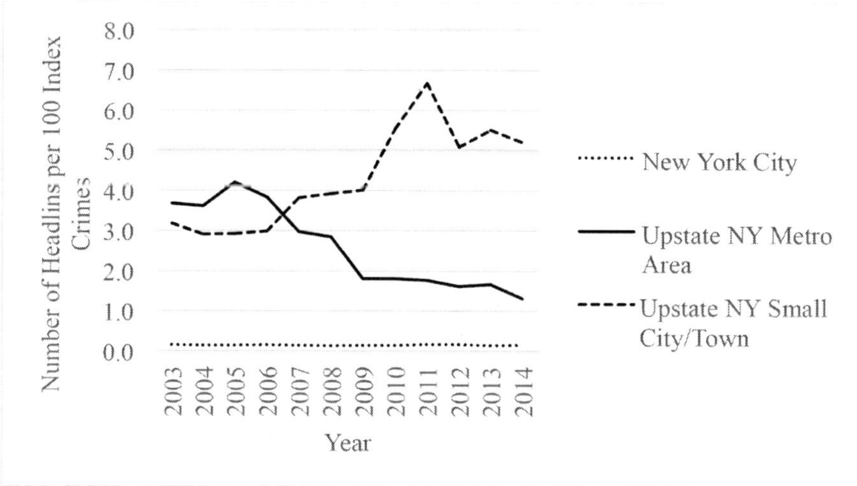

Figure 2.3 Average Number of Crime Headlines per 100 Crime Counts, 2003–2014. *Source*: Author's compilation; see appendix A and Table 1.1 for details.

Media coverage of crimes in the smaller cities and towns of upstate New York rose rapidly from 2006 to 2011, while it dropped steadily after 2005 in the larger upstate metropolitan areas. Comparing the headline counts per one hundred index crimes between 2003 and 2014 indicates the sharp differences among regions. The count is 4.31 in rural upstate newspapers, 2.59 in upstate metropolitan newspapers, and only 0.15 headlines in New York City newspapers. There was on average twenty-nine times more crime coverage in the smaller cities and towns of upstate New York than in New York City, and almost twice as much coverage as in the five larger upstate cities.

These findings contrast with long-standing relationships between the media, crime, and incarceration in other parts of the state. Unlike in the era of mass incarceration, falling crime rates for most of the state have matched not just falling crime coverage but falling incarceration rates. As Figure 2.4 shows, this pattern holds even if we narrow our focus to *drug* reporting—with the notable anomaly yet again of increased visibility and frequency of drug coverage in the newspapers of smaller cities and towns in upstate New York.

News stories in national magazines and newspapers point toward an explanation for these diverging trends: the "meth epidemic," which is supposedly a phenomenon of relatively poor and rural areas. And indeed as Figure 2.5 demonstrates, meth coverage has risen sharply in the post-2009 decarceration period across New York State—and dramatically so for smaller towns and cities.

This requires an inquiry into the relationship between meth reporting and contemporary carceral shifts.

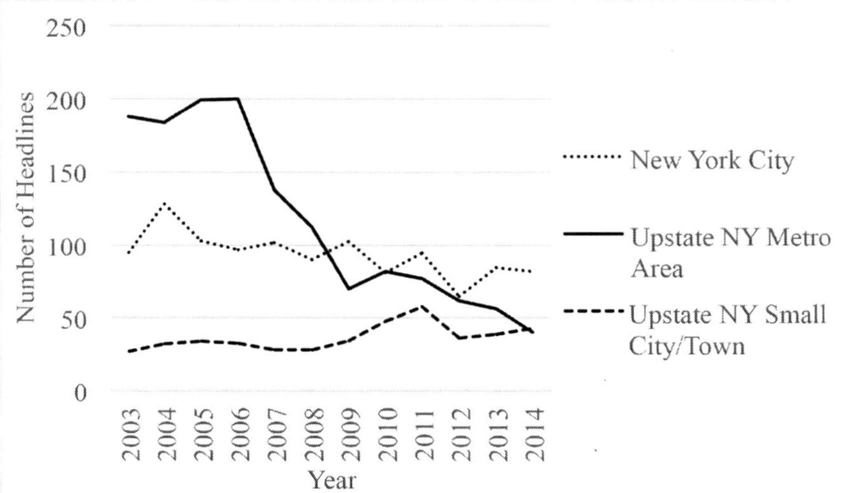

Figure 2.4 Average Number of Drug Headlines, 2003–2014. *Source*: Author's compilation; see appendix A for details.

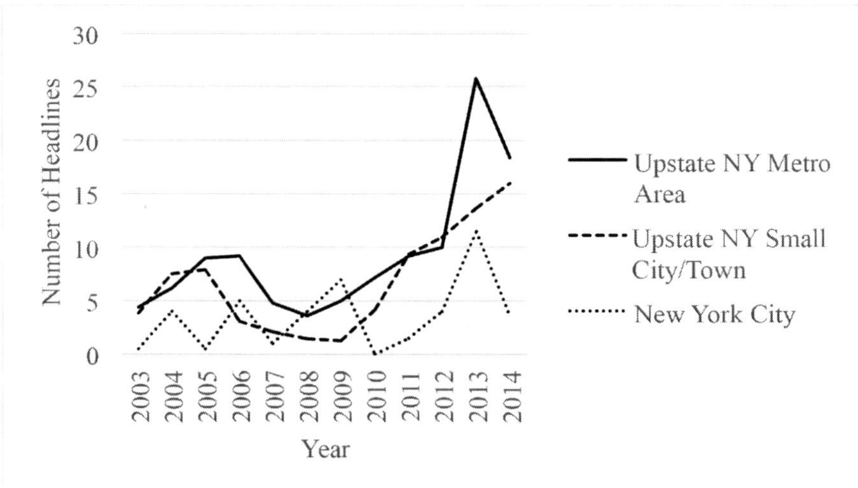

Figure 2.5 Average Number of Meth Headlines, 2003–2014. *Source*: Author's compilation; see appendix A for details.

GOVERNING THROUGH METH

As with previous drug scares, recent meth reporting bears little relation to actual rates of meth use and production: meth use was static or in decline as nationwide reports increased after 2000, while regular meth users are estimated as representing only a fraction of a percent of the US population (SAMHSA 2014; Linnemann 2013; Armstrong 2007; Weidner 2009). Extensive meth coverage nevertheless portrays rural areas as places of risk and insecurity, while promoting widespread surveillance efforts to track users and producers. Travis Linnemann (2013) uses the term "governing through meth" to indicate the expansion of and qualitative shift in law enforcement responses, which have become more reliant on civilian involvement to combat meth.

To understand the significance of meth reporting and these transformations for decarceration, we analyze reporting in Elmira's *Star-Gazette*. The paper is read by the residents of Elmira, a population of 29,000, as well as by residents of neighboring Schuylur, Steuben, and Tioga counties. A search for the keywords, "meth" or "methamphetamine," in the headlines or articles of the newspaper from 2000 to 2015 reveals a rise in meth coverage from 2003 through 2007.

We analyzed the coverage using qualitative media analysis (Altheide and Schneider 2012) to track themes related to meth, crime, and policing as they emerged through the reporting.

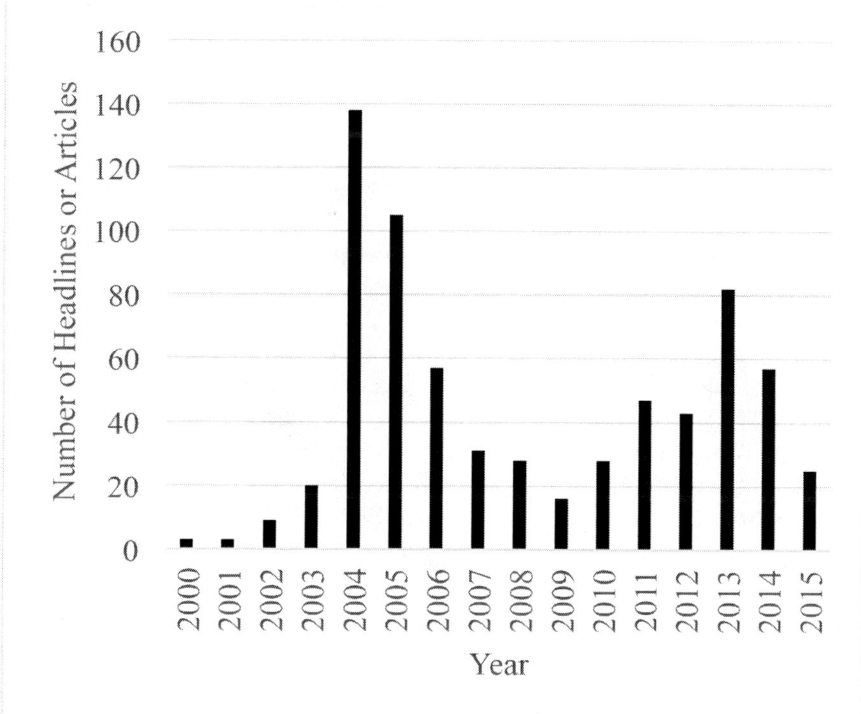

Figure 2.6 Meth Reporting in Star-Gazette, 2000–2015. *Source*: Author's compilation; see appendix A for details.

An analysis of discourse demonstrates how the presentation of meth and meth offenders is developed through statements made by differently positioned claims-makers (Van Dijk 1993; Altheide 2000). In drug scares, journalists and state officials discursively construct (Chermak 1997) drugs as an epidemic tied to criminality and dangerous "outsider" groups (Brownstein 1991; Reinarman 1994; Linnemann 2013; Taylor 2008). In detecting themes we focused on the discursive construction of meth as a social problem. While tracking meth discourse we further investigated how the media's constructions legitimated certain types of responses to the problem.

Our study reveals how meth reporting came to play an essential role in both generating fear and in expanding incarceration in upstate New York. Acting as a platform for state officials and reporters, the media as cultural producers (Linnemann and Kurtz 2014) were able to construct the dimensions by which meth became a criminal issue and thus legitimated certain responses by the police that were key in recent carceral transformations.

METH REPORTING AND "DEGRADING RURALITIES"

The media portrayal of meth as a social problem emerged slowly and then rapidly accelerated.[4] In March 2004, *Star-Gazette* featured a three-day series on drug use in the surrounding area.[5] However, a quantum leap in meth reporting can be attributed to a murder case in neighboring Pennsylvania. On March 31, 2004 Dustin Briggs shot and killed two Pennsylvania sheriff's deputies, Michael Vankuren and Christopher Burgert.[6] The deputies were serving Briggs a fee-related misdemeanor warrant and April Harris a meth-related felony warrant.[7] Briggs fled and was captured after a 36-hour manhunt.

Subsequent case reporting appealed to residents' compassion for the victims' families and friends, while communicating a punitive attitude towards Briggs. Updates on the funeral processions allowed readers to witness the grief and healing of family members, friends, and law enforcement officials.[8] One reporter recalled the immense support Burgert received at his funeral: "hundreds of mourners—many of them police and emergency workers–stood silently Sunday as they waited more than an hour in a wintry mix to enter the funeral home."[9] Simultaneously, reporters conveyed an attitude of retribution by residents. In a typical example, the newspaper reported a local resident saying, "Anyone involved in that (methamphetamine) is asking for trouble and for two people to be killed over it is disgusting. I believe in an eye for an eye, and I hope they sentence him to death."[10] Perhaps unsurprising given this atmosphere, a jury subsequently sentenced Briggs to death.[11]

With the case on the public mind, reporters forged the connection between the killing of the deputies and the overall horrors of meth. As one article stated: "the killing of two deputies is a reminder of how dangerous meth problem [sic] can be."[12] An ingredient of drug scares is the "routinization of caricature," wherein reporters re-craft "worst cases into typical cases and the episodic into the epidemic" (Reinarman 1994, 96). Routine coverage on the case served to construct the image of the typical meth user as, in the words of one article, "violent and out of control."[13]

The meth reporting also constructed a narrative of "degraded, collapsing ruralities" (Linnemann 2013, 44; Bell 2007). Articles spoke of an ominous shift in rural life, transforming Elmira and nearby counties from a safe, close-knit space into one of insecurity, crime, and danger. As a Southport resident was cited saying, "Elmira's changed a lot. . . . It used to be quiet; now big-city problems are happening here. . . . Nothing ever changes back to the way it was. It's gone. Before it gets better, it is going to get worse. . . . It's going to take everybody—the community and the law enforcement."[14] From this reporting it was a short step to depicting the local area as an emerging warzone, akin to the "urban," in need of state-led intervention (Banks 2005; Linnemann and Kurtz 2014; Neocleous 2011).

CONSTRUCTING A SURVEILLANCE NETWORK

The Southport resident's recommendation of collaboration between the community and law enforcement would become an ongoing media theme calling for cost-effective, widespread surveillance efforts to target meth offenders. This would aid in the development of a regional surveillance network that relied on storeowners, landlords, and other community members to perform surveillance duties.

The newspaper played a direct role in encouraging non-state actors to enact surveillance efforts. The newspaper reported on meth informational meetings, led by task forces and police, intended to both warn the public of the dangers of meth and to recruit residents into tracking offenders. As a police officer on the Community Narcotics Enforcement Team told reporters, his series of presentations were meant to recruit "more eyes and ears out there for us."[15] Meetings were held in public spaces like churches and schools, with the newspaper listing times and dates.[16] Reporters further documented the community's approval of such presentations—citing participants' eagerness to join the meth fight.[17]

For those not attending meetings, reporters provided readers with information on how to detect clandestine meth labs. This included listing signs of a potential meth lab: "items disposed along a highway, in a field, forest, etc.,"[18] "bustling activity late at night or in the early hours of the morning," and "refuse left over from the lab."[19] To forge communication between residents and law enforcement, a regional task force planned a "meth tip line," which would, as a senior investigator related, "share locations, descriptions and investigation details between law enforcement agencies in Schuyler, Steuben and Chemung counties."[20] Through these efforts meth reporting was a key participant in the transformation of residents from passive to active agents in state-led social control efforts.

Since ingredients to make meth could be purchased at stores, "the rise of methamphetamines has changed the rules of engagement in the war on drugs,"[21] with the media leading a new front by actively encouraging storeowners and merchants to monitor who purchased meth ingredients (Schuilenburg 2015). An article lauded a campaign called "Merchants Against Meth," which urged storeowners "to put signs in store windows where components used in meth production are found." As the paper reported, the spokesperson for the campaign hoped that this new network would "deter people from buying certain products for drug use and encourage merchants to monitor and track certain purchases." Shops participating in the campaign stretched at the time from neighboring towns to the far reaches of central New York.

Beyond encouraging community participation, reporters praised legislation that would formally draw non-state actors into performing anti-meth surveillance.[22] This included legislation in 2005 that criminalized meth ingredients, placing new responsibility on storeowners for monitoring and tracking meth offenders (Stanley 2007),[23] and authorized prosecution of property owners and landlords for knowingly permitting meth production and dealing on their property.[24] The legislation went further by providing funds for a meth awareness program to, as a state senator claimed, help "state officials and residents spot and report meth making."[25] Reporting thus both encouraged cooperation by residents in the efforts against meth while at the same time praising anti-meth legislation that would formalize community acquiescence to and participation in the war on meth.

FROM SURVEILLANCE TO EXPANSIVE POLICING

These media and policing efforts took concrete form in developing an apparatus of control involving multiple law enforcement initiatives. This permitted the devolution of state authority to local actors, thus minimizing the costs of enforcement through collaboration and technology-driven policing.

Police collaboration through anti-meth task forces was, for example, a common theme in the initial reporting on Briggs.[26] One article covered extensively the first meeting of the Southern Tier anti-meth task force. The meeting was held two days after the shooting of the deputies and was led by Elmira Police Chief James Waters. Attendees included sheriffs from Chemung,

Steuben, and Schuyler counties, New York State Police and "police chiefs from Horseheads, Corning, West Elmira, Elmira Heights and the Southport officer-in-charge." The aim of the task force was to forge departmental alliances and to "call upon the expertise of local agencies, such as public utilities, social services and Narcotics Anonymous" to "prevent the spread of meth." Waters recommended: "We should consider ourselves one (law enforcement) agency as we try to conquer meth."[27] An editorial went so far as to refer to this cooperation as a "meth antidote."[28]

The theme of interagency collaboration in the newspaper continued in coverage of the 2005 Chemung County sheriff's race between then-lieutenant Christopher Moss and retired state police investigator William Mayhew. Moss won on a platform targeting meth, terrorism, identity theft against senior citizens, and the promotion of sharing services among law enforcement agencies. In addition, Moss proposed Chemung County use resources from "Operation IMPACT" [Operation Integrated Municipal Police Anti-Crime Teams], a statewide program that offers grants for law enforcement integration and for intelligence-driven methods to combat crime.[29] Extensive coverage of the sheriff's race helped put themes of anti-meth initiatives and police collaboration on the public mind.

After Moss won the race, the newspaper documented police efforts to combat meth. Moss used an "Operation IMPACT Tools Grant" to initiate "Operation RAM" (Rid the Area of Meth), which was designed to promote community education and to arm law enforcement with crime-fighting technology. The Elmira Police Department created an anonymous police tip line for residents and business owners to call in regarding "suspicious activity." The newspaper listed the Elmira hotline number, while citing residents' approval for the effort.[30] Law enforcement departments were also to be enhanced with electronic technologies to improve surveillance and coordination, including mobile license plate scanners, mobile surveillance cameras, fingerprint scanners, laptop computers in patrol cars, and computer links to the county's 911 command center. A reporter praised growing community efforts and law enforcement for "fighting back with technology."[31]

Officials informed reporters that "Operation RAM" led to various drug arrests. As a reporter relayed: "Moss credited stepped-up police efforts and the public awareness with turning the tide in the [regional] meth war."[32] Furthermore, Elmira Police Chief Scott Drake credited the success of several drug sweeps to a combination of community involvement (with residents calling the crime hotline and sending pictures of suspicious activity to police), advanced police technology, and the targeting by police of "those repeatedly on our suspects' list."[33] Through these successive efforts the media constructed the image of meth as a social problem, promoted expansive, intelligence-led policing across the region, legitimized these efforts, and participated in them.

IMAGINING THE METH OFFENDER

When writing about "the new penology" in 1992, Malcolm Feeley and Jonathan Simon forecast a change in the focus of criminal justice from the rehabilitation of individual moral agents to a concern with "techniques to identify, classify, and manage groupings sorted by dangerousness" (452). This is no longer new today—mass incarceration has expanded this type of policing as a part of monitoring and regulating people of color in urban areas (Wacquant 2001, 2009). As surveillance and policing has expanded upstate, the question arises: how is the meth offender imagined in this new drug war?

On the one hand, although officials described meth users as violent and dangerous, the reporting tended to represent *non-violent* meth users as potentially treatable (Cobbina 2008). An article entitled "A Second Chance" documented a local resident's addiction to and recovery from meth, from his arrest, passage through drug court, to treatment. The reporter highlighted how the drug court offered him a "second chance" and that he recognized the court was there, "to help me, not to harm me . . . I thought I could do it on my own, but I can't do it on my own."[34]

Meth producers and dealers were treated quite differently: the paper represented them as in need of surveillance and management, while a series of editorials declared legislation with these aims necessary to change New York's "wimpy" meth laws.[35] Editorials expressed concern that the Democratic-led House would delay passing anti-meth bills in the Republican-led Senate in an attempt to gain ownership over the initiative with their own anti-meth legislation:[36] "The longer the wait, the more time for meth criminals to have their way."[37] A later editorial added: "Legislative inaction on meth would be a political crime against New Yorkers."[38]

An opinion piece in support of the legislation emphasized this distinction between users and dealers to reconcile the apparent contradiction between the harsh goals of the proposed legislation and recent concerns over the excesses of drug laws:

> After years of trying, lawmakers eased up on punishment for small-time non-violent drug criminals last year—a reform of the so-called Rockefeller drug laws. . . . But that shouldn't be a signal to druggies that the state has gone soft on such crimes. Now that the meth problem has washed across the United States and hit New York and Pennsylvania, legislators need to protect their constituents by giving prosecutors the tools they need to put meth makers and dealers behind bars.[39]

Upon signing the bipartisan 2005 anti-meth legislation, Governor George Pataki echoed the desire to manage and punish meth producers: "It will give law enforcement officials the tools they need to fight this rural New York phenomena. . . . If you're going to manufacture meth, we're going to get you."[40]

In sum, meth producers and dealers were represented as subjects to be managed. Furthermore, while meth is commonly associated with poor, rural whites (Linnemann and Wall 2013; McKenna 2013), drug dealers more generally were often depicted as outsiders, invaders coming in from big cities to disrupt the calm. Above we quoted an anonymous Southport resident as saying, "Elmira's changed a lot. . . . It used to be quiet; now big-city problems are happening here. . . . Nothing ever changes back to the way it was." Arguably, this was an oblique reference to race, where allusions to "big city" problems were a way of associating drugs—and drug dealing in particular—with an urban underclass and people of color (Jenkins 1999, 11).

These symbolic constructions became especially pertinent for local officials when explaining generally low rates of meth production and a declining rate of meth lab busts.[41] As the Briggs case was closing in 2006, for example, the local police predicted, "If the methamphetamine problem hasn't hit the Southern Tier hard yet, it will." A newspaper editorial further embellished by noting, "Fortunately, the spread of meth labs and trafficking has not turned into the full-scale war that it could have . . . [but] . . . law enforcement authorities are a long way from eradicating this dangerous drug from the state."[42]

METH GOVERNANCE, DEVOLUTION, AND JUSTICE DISINVESTMENT

What does the *Star-Gazette* reporting reveal about the relationship between decarceration and meth reporting? How does the media reporting both actively participate in and forecast future trends in carceral formation? Several answers emerge. Comprehensive data show that while official crime rates have steadily declined across the state, crime reporting has accelerated in the small cities and towns of upstate New York. Drug reporting, and especially reporting on meth, has been central to this trend. An in-depth analysis of news stories on meth reveals the effect of the more coverage of meth: it stigmatizes and criminalizes rural areas of New York, producing images of degradation and decay. The Briggs case provides a powerful example of how a single event significantly contributed to this discursive construction.

Framing meth as a threat or plague caused by violent users, producers, and dealers has laid the basis for the diffusion and coordination of surveillance and policing across upstate New York. The newspaper's call for cooperation and collaboration between residents, private actors, and law enforcement, legitimized building a regional surveillance network. The media played an essential role in this production, offering both information on how residents could aid law enforcement efforts and praise for programs and police operations.

Our findings extend beyond, however, a focus on data-driven and intelligence-led policing. As our analysis demonstrates, the continued importance of participation by community members and private actors is central to surveillance processes, while the media act to orchestrate this participation. The media publicized and linked together stories of crime, drug use, and the legitimacy of a police response. The media reported on how community members could identify and report potential meth labs and in this way participated in the surveillance network. This construction of widespread social participation, combined with interagency collaboration, was key in data- and technology-driven policing efforts.

Furthermore, the meth panic removed from public consideration a range of related social issues and problems in upstate New York, including increasing rural poverty, unemployment, agro-corporate political domination, post-industrial depression, and poverty linked to prison closures (see chapter 1; Abel 2014; Armstrong 2007; Tunnell 2006). Reporters' inattention to these social conditions, through an intense focus on managing individual offenders and police actions, facilitates a larger process of justice disinvestment—funds are spent on devolving state authority to locally based, cost-efficient policing and surveillance efforts rather than for the promotion of social welfare.

The meth scare aided in a promotion of fear and insecurity, while expanding massive surveillance as prisons close down. A recognition of the diverse ways in which social control remains entrenched in everyday life, even as mass incarceration wanes, is necessary for a genuine movement towards social and human justice investment. Such an investment in a post-mass incarceration world would certainly give reporters something to write about.

APPENDIX A

Regional definitions: The datasets are created from nineteen newspapers across New York State using two databases: *Newsbank Access World News* and *ProQuest Gannett Newsstand* (see Table 2.1 for more details). Data on "New York City" is compiled from two New York City newspapers, *New York Daily News* and *New York Post* (for our purposes of recording local coverage, *The New York Times* was excluded as a national newspaper).

Data on "Upstate New York Metro Area" is compiled from five newspapers with higher circulation levels (over 50,000 per weekday edition) from the larger cities of upstate New York: *The Times Union* (Albany), *The Daily Gazette* (Schenectady-Albany), *The Buffalo News* (Buffalo), *Rochester Democrat and Chronicle* (Rochester), and *The Post-Standard* (Syracuse). Data for the "Upstate New York City/Town" is compiled from twelve newspapers with lower circulation (under 50,000 per weekday edition) representing the smaller cities and towns of upstate New York: *The Citizen* (Auburn), *The Daily News* (Batavia), *Press & Sun-Bulletin* (Binghamton), *Daily Messenger* (Canandaigua), *The Leader* (Corning), *Star-Gazette* (Elmira), *The Evening Tribune* (Hornell), *Register-Star* (Hudson), *The Ithaca Journal* (Ithaca), *Press-Republican* (Plattsburgh), *Observer-Dispatch* (Utica), and *Watertown Daily Times* (Watertown). See Table 2.1 for further details on circulation and source databases.

Data counts: For Figure 2.1, the visibility and frequency of crime-related stories in the media were tracked by searching for the number of following eight keywords from the headlines (titles) of articles in the newspapers: *murder*, *killing*, *homicide*, *assault*, *robbery*, *theft*, *burglary*, or *rape*. These keywords represent the seven major felony offense categories in the index crime of the New York State Division of Criminal Justice Services: *Murder*, *Rape*, *Robbery*, *Aggravated Assault*, *Burglary*, *Larceny*, and *Motor Vehicle Theft*. Figure 2.1 charts the average number of newspaper headlines related to *crime* in the defined regional categories (see above). Figure 2.3 shows the average number of *crime* headlines per one hundred index crime counts by the different regions (see above). These values can be calculated by the total number of headlines related to *crime* (given the numbers via Figure 2.1) in the newspaper weighed by the count of index crime, released in *New York State Crime Report* (New York State Division of Criminal Justice Services), of the county, where the newspaper is published in, and then multiply 100. In the case of newspapers in New York City, the calculated values cover with New York City five boroughs, which are coextensive with five counties. For Figure 2.4, the visibility and frequency of drug-related stories are observed by searching for the number of the keyword *drug* from the headlines (titles) of articles in the newspapers of the defined regions (see above). For Figure 2.5, the visibility and frequency of meth-related stories in the media are observed by searching for the number of the keywords *meth* or *methamphetamine* in the headlines of articles in the newspapers of the regions as defined above. Figure 2.6 is compiled from searching for the number of the keywords *meth* or *methamphetamine* in the headlines or articles in the newspaper, *Star-Gazette*, in Elmira.

Table 2.1 Newspapers, Circulations, *Crime* Headline Rates, and Accessed Online Databases

Newspaper	*City/Town*	*Circulation (2012)*	*Number of Crime Headlines per 100 Index Crime Counts (Annual Average, 2003–2014)*	*Online Database*
New York Daily News	New York	579,636	0.17	Newsbank Access World News
New York Post	New York	555,327	0.13	Newsbank Access World News
The Times Union	Albany	66,507	3.02	Newsbank Access World News
The Daily Gazette	Schenectady (Albany)	55,719	5.36	Newsbank Access World News
The Buffalo News	Buffalo	147,085	0.87	Newsbank Access World News
Roc. Democrat and Chronicle	Rochester	114,502	0.85	ProQuest Gannett Newsstand
The Post-Standard	Syracuse	78,616	2.85	Newsbank Access World News
The Citizen	Auburn	8,569	4.50	Newsbank Access World News
The Daily News	Batavia	10,500	7.32	Newsbank Access World News
Press & Sun-Bulletin	Binghamton	34,311	1.43	ProQuest Gannett Newsstand
Daily Messenger	Canandaigua	11,255	4.17	Newsbank Access World News
The Leader	Corning	12,818	3.77	Newsbank Access World News
Star-Gazette	Elmira	15,181	3.95	ProQuest Gannett Newsstand
The Evening Tribune	Hornell	6,375	2.15	Newsbank Access World News
Register-Star	Hudson	4,177	3.34	Newsbank Access World News
The Ithaca Journal	Ithaca	9,668	3.02	ProQuest Gannett Newsstand
Press-Republican	Plattsburgh	17,102	4.83	Newsbank Access World News
Observer-Dispatch	Utica	30,645	2.47	Newsbank Access World News
Watertown Daily Times	Watertown	19,268	10.80	Newsbank Access World News

Source: For circulation data, see Alliance for Audited Media (2012).

NOTES

1. We would like to thank Josh Price, John Eason, Brendan McQuade, Andrew Pragacz, Luis González, and Reuben J. Miller for their important comments on this chapter. If not for their suggestions, not to mention independent scholarship, this chapter would not have been possible.

2. Roby, John R. 2015. "Cornwell Claims Victory over Mollen in Tight DA Race." *Press and Sun-Bulletin*, November 4: A.1.

3. Counting of index crime is based on official crime reports submitted by law enforcement agencies to Division of Criminal Justice Service through the Uniform Crime Reporting and Incident Based Reporting program. The FBI and New York State use seven index crime categories as indicators of overall crime trends: violent crimes of murder, rape, robbery, and aggravated assault; and property crimes of burglary, larceny, and motor vehicle theft (for more details, see New York State Division of Criminal Justice Services 2015, 1).

4. Sherman, Brooke J. 2003. "Elmirans Say No to Drugs." *Star-Gazette*, October 12: A.1; Sulat, Christine V. 2003 "A Career Winds Down." *Star-Gazette*, July 13: H.1.

5. Sherman, Brooke J. 2004 "Meth." *Star-Gazette*, March 28: A.1; Sherman, Brooke J. 2004. "Confessions of a Former Drug Dealer." *Star-Gazette*, March 29: A.1; Sherman, Brooke J. 2004. "Answers for Addiction." *Star-Gazette*. March 30: D.1.

6. Sherman, Brooke J. 2004. "Community Expresses Sadness, Concern over Shootings." *Star-Gazette*, April 1: A.9.

7. "Questions and Answers on the Killings." *Star-Gazette*, April 5, 2004: A.6.

8. Wilson, Larry. 2004. "Bradford County's Fallen Deputies." *Star-Gazette*, April 4: A.1.

9. Kingsley, Jennifer. 2004. "Community Lifts Burgert's Family." *Star-Gazette*, April 5: A.1.

10. Kingsley, Jennifer. 2006. "Many Cheer Verdict in N. Tier." *Star-Gazette*, February 8: A.4.

11. "Two Pa. Deputies were Slain Two Years Ago." *Star-Gazette*, March 2, 2006: A.5.

12. "Aftermath of Tragedy." *Star-Gazette*, April 4, 2004: A.8.

13. "Aftermath of Tragedy." *Star-Gazette*, April 4, 2004: A.8.

14. Sherman, Brooke J. 2004. "Community Expresses Sadness, Concern over Shootings." *Star-Gazette*, April 1: A.9.

15. Kingsley, Jennifer. 2004 "Meetings Show how to ID Meth Labs." *Star-Gazette*, August 20: C.1

16. "Bradford County." *Star-Gazette*, April 16, 2004: C.1.

17. Sherman, Brooke J. 2004. "Methamphetamine Presentation Hits Homes." *Star-Gazette*, June 17: A.1.

18. Osgood, George. 2004. "Pa. Police Ask for Help in Fighting Meth Problem." *Star-Gazette*, June 6: C.1.

19. Sherman, Brooke J. 2004 "Meth: Region Fights Back." *Star-Gazette*, April 25: A.1.

20. Sherman, Brooke J. 2004. "Task Force Plans Meth Tip Line." *Star-Gazette*, April 20: A.1.

21. Editorial. 2004. "Fight Meth in N.Y., Reese Tournament." *Star-Gazette*, October 30: A.5.

22. Kingsley, Jennifer. 2005. "Pataki Signs Meth Law in Elmira." *Star-Gazette*, August 11: 15.

23. Much of this legislation was federally mandated in the March 9, 2006 Epidemic Act, included in Title VII of the Patriot Act, including: the regulation of pseudoephedrine based on certifying pseudoephedrine retailers, limiting and regulating purchases of pseudoephedrine, and a logbook for purchases; stricter penalties for retailers in violation of provisions, as well as increasing penalties for production and distribution of meth; increasing government's ability to supervise pseudoephedrine from foreign manufactures; supporting Mexican efforts "to curb meth production"; and efforts to improve environmental regulation and "child-protection" measures, while offering money for anti-meth programs (Stanley 2007).

24. Sherman, Brooke J. 2005. "Winner Calls for Tougher Meth Law." February 1: A.1.

25. "Still Waging a War." *Star-Gazette*, February 20, 2006: A.7.

26. Editorial. 2004. "A Two-State Team." *Star-Gazette*, April 29: A.11.

27. Kingsley, Jennifer. 2004. "Meth Task Force Named in Honor of Deputies." *Star-Gazette*, April 3: A.1.

28. Editorial. 2004. "Meth Antidote." *Star-Gazette*, April 21: A.7.

29. "Moss Cites Campaign Objectives." *Star-Gazette*, August 11, 2005: 12.

30. Salle, Richards. 2007. "Some Stores Stop Selling Drug Items." *Star-Gazette*. February 20: A.1.

31. Richards, Salle E. 2007. "Year in Review: Public Safety." *Star-Gazette*, December 28: C.1.

32. "County Shuts Down Meth Lab." *Star-Gazette*, May 16, 2007: A.1.

33. Richards, Salle E. 2007. "Year in Review: Public Safety." *Star-Gazette*, December 28: C.1.

34. Sherman, Brooke J. 2005. "A Second Chance." *Star-Gazette*, January 9: A.1

35. Editorial. 2005. "An Anti-Meth Dance." *Star-Gazette*, April 21: A.9.

36. Editorial. 2005. "Final Words." *Star-Gazette*, June 7: A.4.

37. Editorial. 2005. "An Anti-Meth Dance." *Star-Gazette*, April 21: A.9.

38. Editorial. 2005. "Crunch Time." *Star-Gazette*, June 16: A.7.

39. Editorial. 2005. "No Reason to Delay." *Star-Gazette*, April 29: A.9.

40. Kingsley, Jennifer. 2005. "Pataki Signs Meth Law in Elmira." *Star-Gazette*, August 11: 15.

41. Sherman, Brooke J. 2005. "N.Y. Sees a Drop in Meth Labs." *Star-Gazette*, August 28: A.9. Additionally, meth lab busts are a flawed way in showing rates of growth, as they may only reflect increased law enforcement efforts (Weidner 2009).

42. Editorial. 2007. "N.Y., Pa. Must Keep Troops Alert in Meth Battle." July 17: OP.1.

REFERENCES

Abel, Jaison R. 2014. "Economic Conditions in Upstate New York." New York: Federal Reserve Bank of New York. Upstate New York Regional Advisory Council Meeting. http://www.newyorkfed.org/aboutthefed/pdf/UNYRAB_June%203_AgendaandPresentations.pdf. Accessed March 30, 2015.

Ahrens, Deborah. 2010. "Methademic: Meth in an Age of Ambivalence." *Florida State University Law Review* 37: 841–900.

Alexander Michelle. 2010. *The New Jim Crow: Mass Incarceration in the Age of Colorblindness*. New York: The New Press.

Alliance for Audited Media. 2012. *FAS-FAX Report* March 2012. http://auditedmedia.com/data/media-intelligence-center/reports-and-tools/reports-library/.

Altheide, David L. 2000. "Tracking Discourse and Qualitative Document Analysis." *Poetics* 27.4: 287–99.

Altheide, David L. and Christopher J. Schneider. 2012. *Qualitative Media Analysis* (2nd ed.). Thousand Oaks, CA: Sage Publications, Inc.

Armstrong, Edward G. 2007. "Moral Panic over Meth." *Contemporary Justice Review* 10.4: 427–42.

Banks, Mark. 2005. "Spaces of (In)security: Media and Fear of Crime in a Local Context." *Crime Media Culture* 1.2: 169–87.

Beckett, Katherine and Theodore Sasson. 2003. *The Politics of Injustice: Crime and Punishment in America* (2nd ed.). Thousand Oaks: Pine Forge Press.

Bell, Michael M. 2007. "The Two-Ness of Rural Life and the Ends of Rural Scholarship." *Journal or Rural Studies* 23.4: 402–15.

Brownstein, Henry H. 1991. "The Media and the Construction of Random Drug Violence." *Social Justice* 18.4: 85–103.

Chermak, Steven. 1997. "The Presentation of Drugs in the News Media: The News Sources Involved in the Construction of Social Problems." *Justice Quarterly* 14.4: 687–718.

Cobbina, Jennifer E. 2008. "Race and Class Differences in Print Media Portrayals of Crack Cocaine and Methamphetamine." *Journal of Criminal Justice and Popular Culture* 15.2: 145–67.

Feeley, Malcolm M. and Jonathan Simon. 1992. "The New Penology: Notes on the Emerging Strategy of Corrections and Its Implications." *Criminology* 30.4: 449–74.

Greene, Judith A., Marc Mauer, Justice Strategies, and N. Y. Brooklyn. 2010. "Downscaling Prisons: Lessons from Four States." Sentencing Project.

Jenkins, Phillip. 1999. *Synthetic Panics: The Symbolic Politics of Designer Drugs*. New York: New York University Press.

Linnemann, Travis. 2013. "Governing through Meth: Local Politics, Drug Control and the Drift toward Securitization." *Crime Media Culture* 9.1: 39–61.

Linnemann, Travis and Don L. Kurtz. 2014. "Beyond the Ghetto: Police, Power, Methamphetamine and the Rural War on Drugs." *Critical Criminology* 22.3: 339–55.

Linnemann, Travis and Tyler Wall. 2013. "'This is your Face on Meth': The Punitive Spectacle of 'White Trash' in the Rural War on Drugs." *Theoretical Criminology* 17.3: 315–34.

Mancuso, Peter J. 2010. "Resentencing after the 'Fall' of Rockefeller: The Failure of the Drug Law Reform Acts of 2004 and 2005 to Remedy the Injustices of New York's Rockefeller Drug Laws and the Compromise of 2009." *Albany Law Review* 73.4: 1535–81.

Mauer, Marc. 2006. *Race to Incarcerate*. New York: The New Press.

McKenna, Stacey. 2013. "'The Meth Factor:' Group Membership, Information Management, and the Navigation of Stigma." *Contemporary Drug Problems* 40.3: 351–385.

Miller, Reuben J. 2014. "Devolving the Carceral State: Race, Prisoner Reentry, and the Micro Politics of Urban Poverty Management." *Punishment & Society* 16.3: 305–35.

Neocleous, Mark. 2011. "'A Brighter and Nicer New Life': Security as Pacification." *Social & Legal Studies* 20.2: 191–208.

New York State Department of Corrections and Community Supervision. 2013. "The New York State Department of Corrections and Community Supervision Announces Prison Reforms That Will Save Taxpayers Over $30 Million Annually Following Decline in Crime Rate and Inmate Population." Albany, NY. http://www.doccs.ny.gov/PressRel/2013/Prison_Closure_Announcement.html.

New York State Division of Criminal Justice Services. 2015. *New York State Crime Report*. http://www.criminaljustice.ny.gov/crimnet/ojsa/indexcrimes/nys-crime-report-2014.pdf.

Parsons, Jim, Qing Wei, Christian Henrichson, Ernest Drucker, and Jennifer Trone. 2015. "End of an Era? The Impact of Drug Law Reform in New York City." New York: Vera Institute of Justice. http://www.vera.org/pubs/drug-law-reform-new-york-city.

Reinarman, Craig. 1994. "The Social Construction of Drug Scares." In *Constructions of Deviance: Social Power, Context, and Interaction*, edited by Patricia A. Adler and Peter Adler, 92–104. Belmont: Wadsworth Publishing Co.

Reinarman, Craig and Harry G. Levine. 1989. "Crack in Context: Politics and Media in the Making of a Drug Scare." *Contemporary Drug Problems* 16: 535–77.

SAMHSA. 2014. "Results from the 2013 National Survey on Drug Use and Health: Summary of National Findings." http://www.samhsa.gov/data/sites/default/files/NSDUHresultsPDFWHTML2013/Web/NSDUHresults2013.pdf.

Schuilenburg, Marc. 2015. *The Securitization of Society: Crime, Risk, and Social Order*. New York: New York University Press.

Simon, Jonathan. 2007. *Governing Through Crime: How the War on Crime Transformed Democracy and Created a Culture of Fear*. New York: Oxford University Press.

Stanley, Patricia. 2007. "The Combat Methamphetamine Epidemic Act: New Protection or New Intrusion?" *Texas Law Review* 39: 379–419.

Taylor, Stuart. 2008. "Outside the Outsiders: Media Representations of Drug Use." *Probation Journal* 55.4: 369–87.

Tunnell, Kenneth D. 2006. "Socially Disorganized Rural Communities." *Crime Media Culture* 2.3: 332–37.

Van Dijk, Teun. 1993. Principles of Critical Discourse Analysis. *Discourse & Society* 4: 249–83.

Wacquant, Loïc. 2001. "Deadly Symbiosis: When Ghetto and Prison Meet and Mesh." *Punishment & Society* 3.1: 95–133.

Wacquant, Loïc. 2009. *Punishing the Poor: The Neoliberal Government of Social Insecurity*. Durham: Duke University Press.

Weidner, Robert R. 2009. "Methamphetamine in Three Small Midwestern Cities: Evidence of a Moral Panic." *Journal of Psychoactive Drugs* 41.3: 227–39.

Williams, Paul and Julie Dickinson. 1993. "Fear of Crime: Read All About It? The Relationship between Newspaper Crime Reporting and Fear of Crime." *British Journal of Criminology* 33.1: 33–56.

Chapter 3

From the Carceral Leviathan to the Police State

Policing Decarceration in New York State[1]

Brendan McQuade

In the mid-1990s, New York City pioneered the use of data-driven policing with the now-famous CompStat program. Since then, data-driven policing has expanded into a broader policing doctrine known as intelligence-led policing (ILP). As decarceration has proceeded in the last decade, administrators in state government have exported these new policing practices to the rest of New York State. The result is the most robust state-level intelligence network in the United States: the large intelligence centers of the NYPD and state police, ten county-level crime analysis hubs, and various interagency programs that share information, produce intelligence, and launch police operations. To make sense of the role of policing in the changes associated with decarceration, I draw on over eight months of fieldwork conducted in 2013 and 2014 and 42 interviews with state troopers, intelligence analysts, municipal police officers, assistant district attorneys (ADAs), probation officers, and others working in intelligence in New York State. I find that intelligence is not just a law enforcement tool. It is a central part of a larger administrative mechanism geared both toward managing the state and governing the population.

As tens of thousands of incarcerated persons are returned to their home communities, the expanded intelligence capabilities of police agencies have extended penal discipline outside the walls of the prison. The declining prison complex, then, is not slouching toward to rehabilitation. Instead of yielding social justice, decarceration is part of a larger reorganization of the state in response to a fiscal crisis and mounting social unrest. The intelligence capacities of state and local governments have grown alongside a more generalized retrenchment in the public sector, including—albeit in complicated and uneven ways—police agencies. At the same time, this increased emphasis on intelligence has facilitated the rise of ILP, a managerial strategy that uses data analysis to supervise police labor and guide proactive police deployments. In this context, this new organization of police supplements mass incarceration with intensified surveillance and new forms of data analysis that feed a series of targeted policing operations. In their fullest development, these programs endeavor to make ambitious interventions to remake social space and prevent future disturbances. The expanding intelligence capacities of police agencies flatten administrative hierarchies. This increased coordination feeds into a process of justice disinvestment: integration of law enforcement agencies offsets fiscal pressures and staff reductions, while, simultaneously, extending the reach of police power. The carceral leviathan is transforming into a diffuse data-driven police state.

This new police state signals more than the institutional ascendency of *the* police, understood as the formal, institutionalized police: the uniformed men (and they are mostly men) who enforce the law. It represents the amplification of a police *power*, a particular form of state power that seeks to promote a certain conception of "good" order in the broadest sense possible. In New York State, the intelligence expansion that proceeded alongside decarceration has integrated the police, courts, community supervision, and other institutions and individuals together in a new set of relationships that extend the reach and scope of police power.

CARCERAL DEVOLUTION AND THE POLICE STATE

The new police state development represents the convergence of interrelated trends. For many decades, the main story has been the sixfold increase in the prison population since the 1970s (Manza and Uggen 2006, 95). The numbers only give a crude measure of change. Mass incarceration has disrupted millions of lives, further marginalized already neglected communities, and, more generally, transformed the United States. Scholars and activists tracked these far reaching effects and offered various interpretations: an evolution of racial control, a "New Jim Crow" (Alexander 2012); a means of warehousing economically superfluous populations (Gilmore 2006); part of a larger political restructuring, where punitive prisonfare and restrictive workfare merge in a new post-welfare, carceral state (Wacquant 2009). These conflict-oriented perspectives converged in the common emphasis on the prison as political instrument, a way of governing the racial other and the restive worker. They positioned the prison—both the institution and the practices and politics surrounding it—as a site of political struggle, not a simple instrument of domination.

While one group focused on the conflictive emergence of a new post-Civil Rights, post-welfare, carceral state, another group took Foucault's suggestive account of the prison as a productive site of disciplinary normalization.

The prison produces prisoners. Disciplinary power produces the individual subject. While this thesis never quite corresponded to the unruly, ill-disciplined reality of actually existing prisons (Alford 2000), Foucault's identification of common patterns of power across a "carceral archipelago" of disciplinary institutions seemed to identify the logic—if not the practice—of power in modern societies. Today many continue this line of argument, tracing the impact of free-floating, future oriented modes of control that are increasingly linked to technological change (Deleuze 1992; Rose 2000; Garland 2001; Haggerty and Ericson 2000).

Of this group, Feeley and Simon's (1992) conceptualization of the new penology was particularly important. They identified the actuarial methods—data-driven processes of risk assessment—that sorted individuals into groups, ranked groups by risk, and recommended the appropriate gradation of custodial control. Instead of individual focus on treatment and rehabilitation, punishment operated across a "custodial continuum," of so-called criminality and deviance managed "according to the degree of control warranted by their risk profiles" (459). This new penology is evident in the varied regimes of risk assessment and monitoring seen across the graduations of custodial power from maximum security to minimum and extending out to community supervision, drug treatment, and, increasingly, a wider network of private sector service providers (Lucken 1997). Significantly, the new penology includes an increased emphasis on "systemic rationality and efficiency" across the custodial continuum, deploying "control strategies rationally . . . [such as] . . . more cost-effective forms of custody and control and in new technologies to identify and classify risk" (Feeley and Simon 1992, 452).

Writing a quarter of a center ago, Feeley and Simon (1992) concluded that the new penology was both a "both cause and effect" of the then-ballooning prison population, suggesting that the growing mass of incarcerated people centered the custodial continuum on the prison. They argued that these actuarial methods had become "permanent features" of criminal justice in the United States (470). In many ways, Feeley and Simon's analysis was prescient, but it was also incomplete. It identified the constitutive logics of power that animated criminal justice but they only considered the practical and discursive coordinates. Here, the more conflict-oriented theories of the carceral state provide the necessary structural and institutional context.

Today, a new wave of reform, increased agitation, and deepening insecurity are combining to reconfigure the carceral leviathan. As formerly incarcerated individuals return to their communities, intelligence expansion in police agencies has collapsed the custodial continuum into interlinked networks of actors across administrative hierarchies. In this way, the term "decarceration" often carries misleading connotations. The formal rollback of the carceral state (the decreasing prison population) obscures a more complex transformation, involving what Reuben Miller (2014) calls "carceral devolution" or "the set of interrelated policies that transfer carceral authority . . . from federal and state-based institutions to local ones" (408).

Before decarceration, the policing sector exhibited these tendencies toward devolution, decentralization, and integration. The failures of criminal justice systems, the commodification of security, and hyper individualist norms have produced a new policing where provisioning of security is no longer the state's sole responsibility and is, instead, the shared task of a linked series of individuals and institutions (Bayley and Shearing 1996; Garland 1996). In this way, decarceration and devolution are revealed as distinct moments in a much longer—and tremendously complex—processes of state formation, where the welfare state and the rigidities of embedded liberalism gradually gave way to the neoliberal state and the renewed quest for a free market utopia. Shifts in penology and policing are part and parcel of these larger changes. The current moment of decarceration is a further reaching alignment. The carceral leviathan, once organized around a central axis of expanding incarceration, is transformed into a "well ordered police state," in which police power not only manages risk but also tries to fabricate social order (Raeff 1983; Neocleous 2001).

This more decentralized and expansive conception of policing harkens back to an older notion of policing (Rigakos and Hadden 2001; Zender 2006). While the prison produces prisoners, the police go further. Policing promotes "good order in the broadest possible sense, including crime and law enforcement but extending through the regulation of trade and commerce, the discipline of labour, the process of education and training, welfare and health, the minutia of social life . . . anything understood as breaching the 'peace'" (Neocleous 2014, 10–11; see also: Foucault 2009, 312–14). In the period of mass incarceration, the individual subject confronted power within different settings on a gradated sequence of custodial encounters: incarceration, reentry, and community supervision. Today, these disciplinary controls cohere around a more fluid logic of policing.

This empowered policing links law enforcement at the federal, state, county, and local levels through intelligence sharing and operational coordination. It extends out to community supervision agencies—probation and parole—which are increasingly becoming important collectors of intelligence and hardening into a pre-emptive form of policing. This process also includes district attorneys, whose mission to prosecute the law has come to blur with the role of *the* police in enforcing it. The resultant policing programs, in their most developed forms, seek to remake individuals and institutions. With the fiscal pressures motivating both decarceration and public sector retrenchment, actuarial methods are used not only to manage external risks but also to ensure the efficient operation of state institutions.

INTELLIGENCE INNOVATIONS IN NEW YORK STATE

The gradual ascendency of police power over custodial forms of control in New York State began with the largest municipality, New York City. In 1994, the NYPD launched computerized statistics (CompStat), the managerial innovation of William Bratton, the NYPD commissioner under tough-on-crime Mayor Rudolph Giuliani. CompStat is built on four principles: (1) timely and accurate crime data, (2) effective strategies, (3) rapid deployment of police resources, and (4) relentless follow up and assessment. The goal of CompStat is to use crime analysis to direct, manage, and evaluate middle management and rank-and-file officers. The system is known to be harsh. During the first year and half of his tenure, for example, Bratton replaced over a third of NYPD's precinct commanders (Walsh and Vito 2005, 60). These reforms enhanced managerial control over police labor as much as they changed the posture of police toward perceived criminality and disorder. In this way, they empowered policing, understood more broadly to connote both the internal management of the state and the external governing of the population.

In the two decades since the first CompStat meetings in New York City, the model has fed into a larger policing doctrine: ILP. Where CompStat compares year-to-date crime data in an effort to set clear crime reduction goals and promote accountability, ILP draws on more sources of data and uses complex analytic methods to identify and target risks. Like CompStat, ILP emphasizes rapid deployment but it tries to move beyond "effective strategies" to the application of preventative measures. Where CompStat focuses on accountability and follow through, ILP tries to shift the posture of policing toward "a top-down management approach" that "uses crime intelligence to objectively direct police resource decisions." These different aspects are visible in chronic offenders programs, a common ILP initiative. In these ways, ILP claims to be a "business model and managerial philosophy where data analysis and crime intelligence are pivotal to an objective, decision-making framework that facilitates crime and problem reduction, disruption and prevention through both strategic management and effective enforcement strategies that target prolific and serious offenders" (Ratcliffee 2008, 6, 83–87).

While ILP conjures up dreams of pre-emptive policing, it is a *managerial* practice oriented toward both the administrative and operational aspects of policing (Maguire and John 2006). One detective (2013) explained:

> We're becoming more surgical. This is the 21st century model of targeted enforcement. We're lean and effective. The previous model was to saturate public space with police. This was ineffective because the criminals would learn when police were going to be in certain places. It was inefficient and expensive

> as well because it required so much manpower. Now, we use intel to dial down on the recidivist 20% that accounts for 80% of crime. This is how we do more with less. Some patrol officers and precinct commanders may not like CompStat and ILP because it means more supervision and control from above but it works and it's the future. There's no fighting it.

In addition to increasing the managerial control within agencies, ILP also entails coordination across agencies. The centerpiece of this effort is intelligence sharing relationships. While small municipalities may not be able to operate a separate intelligence division, their officers can be important collectors of intelligence. Officers at intelligence centers see building these types of relationships—transforming partner agencies personnel into collectors and consumers of intelligence—as central to their work: "We have a business model and we try to excel at customer service so the customer will come back. It is like a McDonalds or Bennigans. Good service builds trust and trust creates real relationships" (Ibid.). While there are problems with implementation, these statements of belief in ILP must be understood as reflections of a new discourse that is animating a real change in power relations.

Starting in 2004, the Division of Criminal Justice Services (DCJS), a statewide office with a broad mission to support criminal justice agencies, began to export CompStat and ILP across the state. DCJS launched Operation Integrated Municipal Police Anti-Crime Teams (IMPACT), a grant-driven interagency partnership between DCJS and the major law enforcement agencies (police departments, district attorney's offices, sheriffs and probation) in the seventeen counties, which, together, account for 80 percent of the crime outside of New York City. Through IMPACT, DCJS disburses grants ranging from $100,000 to over a million dollars that get spread among the various IMPACT partner agencies in a county. From the 2003 to 2013, IMPACT has disbursed over $118 million to the seventeen New York State counties, creating a new state-wide network.[2]

Initially, IMPACT sought to institutionalize the analysis of crime data across the state. The program was explicitly designed to export the emphasis on measurability, results-based initiatives, and accountability associated with the CompStat model to municipalities and counties across New York State. "We saw the value of timely and accurate crime reporting that is paired with rapid reaction and relentless follow up," the former DCJS deputy commissioner (2013) explained. "We wanted to take what had been so effective in the City and apply the model to New York State." The program revolves around two kinds of meetings: monthly IMPACT meetings among all the partners in a county's IMPACT partnership and irregular crime trend meetings between the IMPACT partnership and the DCJS officials. The purpose of both meetings is to tighten the managerial control over police labor, statistically manage police resources, and hold executives accountable for their decisions.

Starting in 2007, DCJS began to use IMPACT funds to set up crime analysis centers (CACs) across the state. This began with the Erie County Crime Analysis in Buffalo and Monroe County Crime Analysis Center in Rochester, and several other counties in the following five years. While DCJS retains some oversight over the CACs it helped found, the program also funds at least six other county-level intelligence taskforces that predate the IMPACT. Twenty years after the first CompStat meeting and a decade since the launch of Operation IMPACT, New York State has developed a criminal intelligence network unlike any other state in the union. Even in counties that lack a CAC, IMPACT-funded crime analysis teams in police departments or sheriff's offices create technically sophisticated intelligence products, and interagency groups regularly meet to share intelligence and plan operations.

The full significance of New York State's robust intelligence network, however, only becomes clear when it is placed in its wider political context. New York State is an early leader in a now nationwide trend toward decarceration. While the pressures from activists and reformers—particularly around drug policy and racial justice—are an important factor, the fiscal crisis of the state remains a major driver of decarceration. Indeed, decarceration and criminal justice reform has become a mainstream policy priority, as seen in the efforts of figures like President Obama and Governor Cuomo to control the process. As a largely top-down process, the policy changes are mostly limited to pragmatic cost-cutting (Gottschalk 2010). It is in this context that we can analyze decarceration as a process of justice divestment: the decrease in the prison population also entails a wider down-scaling of the criminal justice sector and related transfer of state responsibilities down the administrative hierarchy or off-loaded to private entities and individuals.

At the same time, policing is subject to contradictory pressures. The Great Recession appears to have had no impact on police budgets. From 2007 to 2013, the combined operating budgets of all police agencies in the United State increased by over 15 percent from $55.4 billion to $64.1 billion (Reaves 2010, 6; Reaves 2015, 15). In New York State, total investment in policing increased from $8.4 billion in 2009 to $9.3 billion 2012 (Kyckelhahn 2015a; 2015b). At the same time the overall level of investment in police agencies increased, police employment has decreased. Across the United States, total police employment has dropped by over 11.5 percent, from 1,017,953 in 2007 to 899,212 in 2014 (Federal Bureau of Investigation 2007; 2013). While the national data tells a story of sharp decline, the change in New York State has been minimal.[3]

This nominal decrease obscures a more complicated picture. In this period, total number of police officers has declined by 1,432, a drop of more than 2 percent. The two largest police agencies in the state, the NYPD and the New York State Police (NYSP), account for over one third this decrease. The NYPD and NYSP have also cut civilian employment by 5 and nearly 30 percent respectively. The decline in police employment across the state would be more pronounced were it not for a 6 percent increase in civilian police employment in all police agencies excluding the NYPD and NYSP. This latter category is the only area of meaningful growth in the police employment (Division of Criminal Justice Services 2015). While the data made available by the state does not break down the civilian employment further, the trend suggests that Operation IMPACT and the larger diffusion of CompStat and ILP out of New York City could be fueling the increase of civilian employees, as smaller jurisdictions hire analysts and expand their intelligence capabilities. Moreover, the general trends—increasing investment in policing and decreasing numbers of police officers—also suggest that intelligence expansion may be creating lean, data-driven police agencies. Are machines and intelligence analysts replacing officers?

In this context, the managerial aspects of CompStat and ILP are especially important. The ascendency of police power and its amplification by actuarial methods increases the disciplinary regulation of police labor. Police agencies are being asked to do more work with fewer officers. They are offsetting increased workload and staff reductions with two related strategies, both of which are a direct result of the export of the NYPD's innovations: (1) leveraging interagency partnerships, and (2) using information technology and data analysis to manage resources. These strategies are remaking police agencies and changing the practice of policing, albeit in conflictive and uneven ways (McQuade 2016). The interagency relationships that surround ILP expand the reach of large police agencies, effectively deputizing smaller agencies as adjuncts of larger departments. The increased emphasis on intelligence within police agencies and the premium placed on collaboration that comes with ILP necessarily changes the practical nature of policing. Risk assessments impinge upon the discretion of police officers, probation and parole officers, and others in the criminal justice system. Targeted operations have come to replace the saturation of public space. Ambitious programs to regulate individuals and communities replace a narrow focus on crime control and arrest.

NEW YORK STATE'S INTELLIGENCE SHARING NETWORK

While each IMPACT partnership develops unique programs, DCJS has standardized a basic structure related to the gathering, sharing, and analysis of intelligence in every IMPACT county. This system is comprised of three pillars: (1) field intelligence officers for the collection of human intelligence,

(2) crime analysis whether in the form of a crime analysis team or a larger CAC, and (3) monthly IMPACT meetings for interagency coordination and collaborative development of ILP initiatives.

Operation IMPACT funds at least one field intelligence officer in every IMPACT jurisdiction. These officers, usually placed with the largest municipal police department or the sheriff's office, are important collectors of intelligence. The core of their work is informal interviews called "debriefings" with every person who comes through the county jail and arrestees of interest. Generally, field intelligence officers ask about drugs, guns, and gangs. If the individual shares information relevant to ongoing investigations, the field intelligence officer will contact the officer investigating the other case. When confirmed and vetted by other sources, intelligence gathered from debriefings can be used in products that are disseminated across the county, region, and state.

Depending on the size of the jurisdiction, the number of field intelligence officers and the amount of emphasis placed on debriefings, an individual field intelligence officer will do between 500 and 1,000 debriefings a year.[4] One Sheriff's Department in New York's Mid-Hudson Region has four field intelligence officers in the law enforcement division and ten "debriefers" in the corrections division. The detective sergeant (2014) who oversees the intelligence operations said that each these officers do about 250 debriefings year, bringing the total number of debriefings done in this jurisdiction to approximately 3,500. The greater goal is, in the words of this officer, "to turn every debriefed individual into a confidential human source, whether it be operational or intelligence only." In this case, "operational" means an informant who is actively involved in police operations as a covert agent that may be asked, for example, to develop a relationship with a known drug dealer. An informant that provides intelligence only simply reports potentially useful information to his or her law enforcement handler but is not directed to collect intelligence as part of an investigation. Officially, this sheriff's office has 12 active informants and 22 inactive ones.

These debriefings bring an important new facet to routine arrests. It is no longer just the start of an individual criminal justice proceeding but an moment of intelligence collection that feeds into a wider network of intelligence sharing and nested systems—local, county, regional, statewide—of situational awareness and risk assessment. Debriefings offer an opportunity for law enforcement to peer inside the often opaque realities of everyday life through creating informants, finding new avenues to work cases, and obtaining insights on their jurisdictions. They signal yet another way intelligence expansion has enlivened and extended police power, transforming individuals outside of criminal justice agencies into agents of the police state.

Crime analysis is another pillar of the program. In every IMPACT county, DCJS funds at least one crime analyst who provides data analysis and crime mapping. This work has an important managerial aspect to it. Crime analysts identify patterns and hotspots. They help police executives decide how to deploy police resources, whether in the form of routine patrols or more targeted operations. As the police chief (2013) of a small city with unusually high crime rates explains: "The most effective policing we've ever done is ILP, incident-based policing. [This city] doesn't have a lot of public funds to go around. The crime analyst is a force multiplier. I need to be able to see those hotspots and send my guys there." This point was echoed by another police chief (2013) in one New York's largest cities: "I do use crime data to manage the department. It tells me where I need to focus the investigative division. It drives the patrol division. What they do is directly the result of the information and intelligence they develop."

Regular interagency meetings are the third pillar of IMPACT. These meetings are co-chaired by the primary jurisdiction's chief or commissioner of police and the county district attorney. Representatives from the county Sheriff's Office and Probation Department, NYSP, the state's Department of Corrections and Community Supervision, which includes parole, also attend. In certain counties, federal law enforcement agencies—the Federal Bureau of Investigation, the Bureau of Alcohol, Tobacco, Firearms and Explosives, the US Marshal's Service, and the United States Attorney's Office—also participate. These meetings have three purposes: developing a common awareness of crime trends across agencies, sharing information, and planning multi-jurisdictional operations.

The quality of the meetings varies across the 17 IMPACT counties with some interviewees describing them as an empty formality and others lauding their utility for all parties. Although friction remains at the executive level, all my interviewees acknowledged that IMPACT increased interagency coordination. Even the interviewee who was most critical of the executive level IMPACT meetings, a police chief (2013) in the capital district, had this to say: "If IMPACT has worked anywhere, it's for the cops at the level of operations. Now, our guys are talking to the Sheriff about burglary rings in the county and the city. We have State Police [Community Narcotics Enforcement Team] in here all the time working with our narcotics guys. IMPACT broke down these barriers. When it comes to pencil pushers like me at the top, things get more political but, for the guys that actually fight crime, IMPACT has changed the way we operate." In a time of austerity and state retrenchment, this chief sees the program as an important source of "budgetary relief by covering for the salaries of positions like field intelligence officer and domestic violence investigator. It's been brilliant in that it has forced agencies to work together. Internally, it's made us realize how much more we need to communicate within the department so it's opened us up and helped make us more efficient."

Taken together, Operation IMPACT has exported New York City's policing innovations upstate and created an integrated intelligence sharing network. In so doing, the state has institutionalized the collection of human intelligence and the analysis of crime data, while increasing coordination across agencies. On an institutional level, IMPACT has forged links across institutional hierarchies, enabling individual agencies to make up for staff reductions by pooling resources and coordinating operations. With this system of intelligence sharing and interagency coordination in place, ILP becomes a shared managerial practice that seeks to bring greater efficiency to the criminal justice system. This intelligence sharing system also operates as conduit of police power, a means through which to promote "good order" within government. The ascendency of police power also changes how the state governs populations. Here, the operational side of ILP is essential.

POLICING DECARCERATION

This new policing is deployed to govern a precarious population that is increasingly unbound from disciplinary institutions, whether the prison, the school, or the factory. The new police state creates a new set of relationships among the shrinking prison, high-tech police precincts, and poverty stricken neighborhoods. In this context, the contemporary police state goes beyond managing the racialized, socially excluded and potentially disruptive populations by warehousing them in prisons. It reorganizes criminal justice around an actuarially-empowered form of policing in an attempt to fabricate social order, remaking subjects and spaces deemed threatening. In New York State, the new police state takes practical form in a series of operations—warrant sweeps, compliance checks, chronic offender initiatives and saturation patrols—that attempt to extend penal discipline outside of prison walls and use police power to normalize subjects in place.

Partnerships between police agencies and probation or parole harden community supervision programs into a form of pre-emptive policing. To avoid a prison sentence or to be released from one, probationers and parolees forfeit freedom of movement and association with others. The terms of probation or parole will often include more specific requirements.[5] A violation of these terms can result in the revocation of community supervision and a return to prison. As part of these arrangements, probation and parole officers keep detailed records about their clients' whereabouts, histories, and associations. Probation and parole officers are also empowered to conduct home visits and can search clients without a warrant. In warrant sweeps and compliance checks, police officers will leverage the detailed records and enhanced powers to extend the enforcement of orders of protection. A probation officer

(2014) in New York State explained: "We have great relationships with the police department. We have so much more information than they do. Their records are limited to basically just criminal histories, if they're lucky their intel or detective bureau will have a file on someone but that's hardly assured. We can give them a lot more: where they live, where their family members live, where they work."

Both compliance checks and warrant sweeps are attempts to make enforcement of community supervision continuous. They target individual subjects who are already "known" by the state and subjected to a formal disciplinary regime but they attempt to transform enforcement into a general condition and not just a series of scheduled meetings with probation or parole officers. In this way, compliance checks and warrant sweeps represent an intermediate point between the custodial logic of mass incarceration and the ascendant police power associated with decarceration.

After ten years of IMPACT, these operations have become common across the state. In reference to compliance checks, one probation officer (2014) explained that, "For IMPACT details, we will partner up with the police department or Sheriff and do compliance checks on my higher risk cases." In Monroe County, for example, the probation field intelligence officer conducted 185 of these home searches in 2013. In Erie County, the probation field intelligence officer performed 197 compliance checks, including 153 with the aid of the Buffalo Police Department's Canine Unit (Division of Criminal Justice Services 2013, 14, 16, 19).

Warrant sweeps are also a fixture of policing throughout New York State. In 2006, the US Marshalls launched "Operation Rolling Thunder," a sweep program for outstanding federal warrants. By 2008, six IMPACT jurisdictions participated in the effort (Division of Criminal Justice Services 2008, 10; Kava 2008).[6] In 2009, the year after DCJS set up set up its first CAC, the Buffalo-based Erie County Crime Analysis Center (ECAC), DCJS began organizing sweeps for state warrants. The Erie County IMPACT partnership launched a pilot program, "Violent Offender Interdiction Collaborative Effort" or Operation VOICE. The sweeps started with crime analysis to identify everyone with outstanding warrants in and around a crime hotspot on Buffalo's East Side. To execute the sweep, the Buffalo Police Department deployed its IMPACT-funded mobile response unit: "a proactive unit that consists of Buffalo police officers and New York State troopers who patrol areas of the city based on real-time crime information provided by the Erie Crime Analysis Center." Over the course of a 90-day period, 147 people "were systematically arrested and debriefed" (Division of Criminal Justice Services 2009, 24, 40). Since the inception of IMPACT in 2004, the Buffalo police have executed 39,734 warrants, including 4,855 in 2013 alone (Division of Criminal Justice Services 2013, 13).

Like warrant sweeps and compliance checks, chronic offender programs and saturation patrols are a pre-emptive policing effort. Unlike warrants sweeps and compliance checks, however, they are not premised on a legal mandate that *obliges* a state intervention. Instead, chronic offender programs target individuals on the basis of intelligence. Analysts use "specific and objective, data-led criteria to identify individuals who should be targeted" (Division of Criminal Justice Services 2008, 11). These programs bring together police agencies and district attorney/county prosecutor's offices to keep perceived "career criminals" off the streets at all costs, even it if means prosecuting them for minor offenses, which result in short sentences at a county jail. As a point of doctrine, ILP emphasizes "disruption and prevention through both *strategic management* and effective enforcement strategies that target prolific and serious offenders" (Ratclifee 2008, 182; emphasis mine). Chronic offender initiatives can potentially replace lengthy prison sentences with constant surveillance and aggressive policing, punctuated by brief stays in county jails.

Saturation patrols are an even more generalized iteration of the same doctrine of pre-emptive policing. Saturation patrols are similar to chronic offender initiatives in that they are driven primarily by intelligence analysis. There is no legal mandate to saturate a given area with an intensified police presence. Instead, police executives use crime mapping to plan data-driven deployments to combat specific "hotspots." While these efforts are increasingly part of routine police administration, they also can take on an exceptional character in response to perceived surges in crime, usually centered on gun violence, drug dealing, or property theft. Saturation patrols often involve "enhanced prosecution."[7] In contrast to compliance checks and warrant sweeps, chronic offender initiatives and saturation patrols represent clear dominance of policing over custodial forms of power. These programs target perceptions of generalized risk—"crime hotspots"—not individual subjects. In their generalized policing of social space, they attempt to produce the domestic tranquility that allows for governing "in peace."

In all IMPACT jurisdictions, DCJS encourages the development of chronic offender lists. Unlike other ILP operations, ADAs will be involved in the creation of the chronic offender lists, the intelligence products that provide the basis of these operations. Due to tensions between police agencies and district attorney's offices regarding these programs, however, the details of these chronic offender programs are not widely shared.[8] One of the most celebrated and publicized versions of these programs, the Chronic Offender Recognition and Enforcement (CORE) Program in Onondaga County provides an example of how these programs work and why they are controversial. The programs uses intelligence produced at the Onondaga Crime Analysis Center (OCAC) to "target the estimated 8 percent of criminals who commit about

80 percent of the crimes in the community" (O'Hara 2008). The program was initially a great success on its own terms. All of the original twenty-six chronic offenders who were on the CORE list were arrested and nineteen were prosecuted and convicted (Division of Criminal Justice Services 2013, 11). "The first CORE list we had was really successful in terms of prosecuting them federally or locally," an assistant district attorney (2013) told me "but the second CORE list, once you start getting the assholes off the street, the target rich environment becomes less and less robust. Soon, you're questioning how chronic these guys are. If your program is successful, it is going to end."

By the time of the third CORE list in 2010, interagency conflict had sunk the program. "Core I and Core II were extremely successful. Core III started to take a turn and that's when the political stuff starting coming in"; a police captain (2013) in a supervisory position with the OCAC explained, "We started to see that we were arresting these guys and they weren't getting any different treatment than any normal person would go through the system. Through a series of meetings it was stated that we are not going to treat these guys any different than anyone else. So that didn't sit well with the law enforcement side of things." From the perspective of the DA's office, the police expected the prosecutors to bend the rules of criminal justice:

> You can't go into a court and tell a judge "This is a CORE offender. You need to treat him more harshly." That goes against every grain of the American criminal justice system. Trying to explain that to the police is a different story. "We know he's a bad guy." Well, OK, that's great. We need proof . . . prosecutors have an ethical obligation, OK? All the stuff you've read in the IMPACT reports about the enforcement side of things needs to be tempered by claims of organizations like the Innocence Project, who say that all these people have been wrongfully convicted because of overzealous police or because of police or prosecutorial misconduct. . . . Our job is not to prosecute and convict people that the police arrest. Our job to evaluate a case and ensure that (A) the person is the right person to prosecute and (B) that we have the right evidence to convict him and survive an appeal down the round. (Assistant District Attorney 2013)

Similar tensions complicated other chronic offender initiatives, in other counties. As a result, the Office of Public Safety, the component of DCJS that oversees IMPACT, started to compile its Persistent Chronic Offender Lists in 2011. The statewide lists provide police agencies with the intelligence necessary to mount targeted investigations of chronic offenders, thus neutralizing tensions between police agencies and district attorney's offices and allowing the pre-emptive policing of "chronic offenders" to continue.

In their simplest form, saturation patrols are a product of the managerial aspects of ILP. Indeed, they are the foundation of the operational end of

IMPACT, which started, in 2004, with crime analysis driving "blue and gray patrols" or joint patrols of state police and municipal police officers and/or sheriff's deputies (Deputy Commissioner 2013). Some IMPACT partnerships, however, take saturation patrols a step further and target them on a specific crime and connect them to efforts at enhanced prosecution. "Operation Speeding Bullet" in Albany County is a good example. The operation involves the Albany County Crime Analysis Center, the police department, sheriff's office and the district attorney's office. Like other ILP initiatives, "Operation Speeding Bullet" begins with crime analysts conducting a spatial and temporal breakdown of shots fired. On the basis of the resultant crime maps, police will patrol the areas. The officers to look to both prevent future shootings *and* question known persons of interests connected to past shootings. In this latter capacity, the saturation patrols gather human intelligence that can lead to seizure of illegally possessed guns. From 2008 to 2011, these saturation patrols led to the recovery of between 90 and 120 guns per year (Albany Police Department 2012; Director 2013). The resultant arrests are referred to an IMPACT-funded Gang and Gun Prosecutor in the district attorney's office, who operates on call 24 hours a day, 7 days a week. After the arrest, the case is heard by a grand jury instead of a normal preliminary hearing with judge. These measures allow the prosecutor to set a higher bail. With the increased resources made available through Operation IMPACT and the heightened coordination through Operation Speeding Bullet, Albany County now moves a gun case from arrest to conviction in average time of 45 days. In the period from July 2013 to June 2014, the district attorney's office "prosecuted almost 50 felony firearm cases with more than two dozen open cases during the grant year" (Albany Police Department 2014).

These programs are not without their internal problems, as the example of CORE attests. Even with such friction, a general trend is clear. In the new police state, the parole officer working in partnership with the sheriff's deputy replaces the corrections officer and the prison bars. Instead of prisons, the new police state quarantines the socially excluded and economically redundant in the decaying edifices of neglected neighborhoods, where the most conspicuous presence of the state is the surveillance camera and the squad car.

This arrangement is not without tensions. Politics mediate policing, including continued demands for austerity, pressure from social movements, internal professionals struggles, and so on. Currently, the political winds have shifted toward reform. In this context, the internal jockeying to define law enforcement professions from within are important. These indeterminate struggles can produce further openings for change or provide the policy solutions to slow the process. Within the world of domestic intelligence and ILP, there are several points of conflict. In 2013 and 2014, I found that chiefs of crime-ridden, economically marginal, small- to medium-sized cities were most likely to resist ILP in the name of community policing. Probation and parole officers will also offer resistance on similar grounds (McQuade 2016). Today, this balance of forces appears to be changing. Community policing is the policy solution embraced by reformers.

LOOKING FORWARD TO COMMUNITY POLICING: REFORM OR RETRENCHMENT?

Significant decarceration is heralded by liberals as a return to a rational, rehabilitative, and much smaller prison system. When we focus on policing, a different narrative emerges: the transformation of the carceral leviathan into a new, data-driven police state. Polite conversation among the reformers has ignored this massive intelligence expansion with its networks of informants and aggressive operations. Instead, the discourse of community policing dominates the conversation. In May 2015, President Obama announced the recommendations of the Presidential Task Force on Twenty-First Century Policing: renewed emphasis on community policing and more oversight and training, all facilitated by new technology and the expanded use of intelligence. That same month, Attorney General Loretta Lynch launched a national community policing tour to highlight model programs and promote a $163 million grant program to implement the task force's suggestions (McQuade 2015a). The return to community policing signals the ascendency of a group of reformers, who have long advocated incorporating ILP within an overarching strategy premised on community engagement (Innes 2006; Innes et al. 2009).

This seeming shift actually complements the ongoing ascendency of police power. Community policing deputizes third parties—neither state agencies nor perceived criminals—as intelligence collectors and partners in the projection of police power. The result is, as I have argued elsewhere, a more integrated authoritarianism (McQuade 2015b). In New York State, some existing programs situate ILP operations within a larger strategy premised on community outreach and collaborative problem solving. By way of conclusion, I contend that these programs represent the most ambitious and far reaching applications of police power. Where other ILP initiatives simply coordinate operations among different state agencies, these programs encourage community members to become self-directed intelligence reporters. They endeavor to reorganize "private" social spaces to amplify police power. They portend a dark future beyond mass incarceration but still far from abolition democracy.

The Operation Safe Homes-Safe Streets of the Albany County District Attorney (DA) exemplifies how community policing complements the ongoing transformation of the carceral leviathan into a police state. The initiative brings the DA, Albany Police Department (APD), and the Albany Crime Analysis Center (ACAC) together with landlords to uproot a perceived source of urban disorder: a complex of blighted properties, negligent landlords, disreputable tenants, and criminalized goods. The program extends beyond mere law enforcement. It is a state-led political project to remake social space—and it is driven by actuarial systems and related intelligence sharing partnerships. As a first step, intelligence analysts identified a 77-block area that accounted for more than half of the crime in Albany County (Division of Criminal Justice Services 2010, 9). The analysts created "premise histories" of 165 properties in the area and scored their relative risk, identifying eleven high risk or "Code Red" properties. From here, the intelligence sharing relationships that surround the ACAC facilitate a coordinated effort to move from monitoring to execution of warrant and eviction (Albany Police Department 2010a).

While other criminal justice agencies focused on the eleven Code Red Properties, the DA compelled landlords to join the trespass affidavit program, which requires landlords to provide lists of all tenants, post "No Trespassing" signs, grant police full access at all hours, and permits police to search abandoned property at will. The "No Trespassing" signs encourage residents to report suspicious behavior (Ibid.). As part of the program, a dedicated assistant district attorney (ADA) trains property owners to screen tenants in order to "identify criminal behaviors." The ADA also provides landlords with sample "zero tolerance leases," which empower landlords with considerable discretion to evict the tenant. The program not only invites landlords to evict tenants, it also punishes landlords who do not. Under Safe Homes-Safe Streets, the DA, APD and partner agencies will evict tenants if the landlord fails to do so—and subjects landlords to fines of up to $5,000 plus legal fees. Over time, landlords who resist the program are subject to more intense supervision. As part of Safe Home-Safe Streets, analysts will create "property owner trees" for "repeat offender landlords." They hope such efforts to map out other properties will "reveal a pattern and/or history of criminal activity," and identify "property owners that are working directly with those committing offenses." In other words, intelligence analysts will widen the net and attempt to identify the vulnerabilities of uncooperative landlords (Albany Police Department 2010b).

By the end of 2010, the DA, APD and other agencies had executed warrants on and evicted tenants from the eleven houses originally designated "Code Red." The apparent success of the program convinced Albany County to conduct risk assessments of every property in the county. While the determining reach and effects of these programs requires more research, it is clear that Safe Homes-Safe Streets goes beyond law enforcement and attempts to produce "good order." The scope of the program is impressive. In the five years of the program from 2009 to 2014, the APD has shut down nineteen "Code Red" properties and executed 100 evictions, while the DA's trespass affidavit program has trained over 770 landlords and registered over 1,000 properties (Albany Police Department 2014). These efforts remove the incentive for landlords to look the other way and collect rents from tenants that sustain themselves through the clandestine and criminalized trades (i.e., drugs). Through threat of fines and increased monitoring, the program compels landlords to become part of a larger network of police power. In this way, the trespass affidavit program enlists landlords in the operations of police power. Through these combined efforts, Safe Homes-Safe Streets collapses the custodial continuum into an integrated assemblage of police power. The program seeks to partner criminal justice agencies with landlords, tenants, and area residents in a series of programs that effectively deputizes landlords and tenants as agents of administrative surveillance, extending the reach of police power.

Safe Homes-Safe Streets is one of the more dramatic examples of the new data- and intelligence-driven policing practices being institutionalized across New York State. Taken together these recent innovations have provided a central pillar to the process of decarceration. The tendencies on display in Safe Homes-Safe Streets—actuarial risk assessments, interagency information sharing, and expansive multiagency operations that extend far beyond law enforcement—are increasingly common across the state and institutionalized in a series of other programs. These examples speak to the broader reorganization of criminal justice institutions that has transformed the custodial continuum into a new police state. Rather than a distinct and escalating sequence of risk assessment and state intervention from solitary confinement in a supermax to probation, there is an increasingly coordinated operation of police power across these seemingly distinct institutional domains. As prison populations contract or otherwise level off, a new police state takes precedent in the administration of criminal justice and the wider governing of the population.

NOTES

1. I would like to thank Bill Martin, Josh Price, John Eason, Andrew Pragacz, Chungse Jung, Luis González, Kevin Revier, and Reuben J. Miller for their helpful commentary. In particular, I would like to thank Bill and Josh for their work conceptualizing and coordinating this collective research project.

2. In 2014, Operation IMPACT was renamed Gun-Involved Violence Elimination (GIVE).

3. For a point comparison, the national breakdown of changes in police employment is, of course, uneven but the decline is obviously dominant. In New York State, total police employment decreased by just 2 percent of a percent from 92,202 in

2007 to 90,077 in 2014. New York is the fourth largest state in the union by population. In comparison with other states in the top five, New York's experience is mirrored by California, which saw 2 percent decline (from 120,976 to 118,491) in the period from 2007 to 2014. In the other states, the decline is very dramatic. Total police employment dropped in Texas by 28 percent (from 84,403 to 60,056) in Florida by 18.5 percent (from 74,562 to 60,714), and in Illinois by 35.7 percent (from 53,537 to 34,425).

4. These numbers are generated from four sources: an interview with a field intelligence officer at a sheriff's department in an Upstate New York county who said he does seventy to eighty debriefings a month, an interview with police chief who said his field intelligence officers will do "as many as 1000 debriefings in a year," an interview with another police chief who said his field intelligence officers will do "around 500 or 600 debriefings a year," and the Binghamton Police Department 2010 Annual Report which reported that the department's field intelligence officer did 566 debriefings. See: Binghamton Police Department, *Annual Report, 2010*, http://www.binghamton-ny.gov/sites/default/files/documents/files/2010%20Annual%20Report%20web_0.pdf (Accessed July 20, 2013): 65; Field Intelligence Officer, Interview by author, Phone Interview, Binghamton New York, June 3, 2014; Police Chief, Interview by author, Personal Interview, Tape Recorded, City in New York's Mid-Hudson Region, July 19, 2013; Police Chief, Interview by author, Personal Interview, Tape Recorded City in New York's Finger Lake Region, August 22, 2013.

5. Other requirements include avoiding contact with certain people, including other people convicted of a felony, remaining employed, staying sober, submitting to regular drug tests, abiding by a curfew, participating in treatment for substances abuse, receiving psychological counseling or performing community service.

6. Among them, the Oneida and Erie Counties were the earliest and most enthusiastic participants. In 2008, multi-jurisdictional teams in both counties conducted a series of warrant sweeps in a two week span, apprehending 106 persons in Oneida County and 140 in Buffalo (Division of Criminal Justice Services 2008, 10; Kava 2008).

7. Generally, the "enhanced prosecution" means that a district attorney or county prosecutor will not accept plea deals and instead will try to secure a conviction for the harshest charges possible. It also can connote the application of specialized legislation that require mandatory minimum sentences for particular offenses.

8. Many interviewees did not want to discuss the programs in depth. The sharply fought battles between senior personnel in municipal police departments and sheriff's offices, on one side, and district attorney's offices on the other, were "too political" to discuss.

REFERENCES

Albany Police Department. 2014. "Operation IMPACT X: Agency Budget Narrative for the Period July 1, 2013 through June 30, 2014." Albany Police Department.

Albany Police Department. 2012. "Response IX (part B): Strategy for Address Firearm Related Crimes." Albany Police Department.

Albany Police Department. 2010a. "Worksheet 2, Strategy for Part 1 and Firearm-Related Violent Crime: Targeting Crime Hot Spots/Disrupting Drug Markets." Albany Police Department.

Albany Police Department. 2010b. "Worksheet 2, Strategy for Part 1 and Firearm-Related Violent Crime: Targeting Firearm-Related Crime." Albany Police Department.

Alexander, Michelle. 2012. *The New Jim Crow: Mass Incarceration in the Age of Colorblindness*. New York: The New Press.

Alford, Fred. 2000. "What Would it Matter if Everything Foucault Said About Prison were Wrong? Discipline and Punish After Twenty Years." *Theory and Society* 29, no. 1 (February): 125–46.

Assistant District Attorney, County in Central New York. 2013. Interview by author. Phone Interview. Tape Recorded. Binghamton, New York. June 26.

Bayley, David H. and Clifford D. Shearing. 1996. "The Future of Policing." *Law and Society Review* 30, no. 3 (February): 585–606.

Binghamton Police Department. 2010. *Annual Report, 2010*. Binghamton. http://www.binghamton-ny.gov/sites/default/files/documents/files/2010%20Annual%20Report%20web_0.pdf (Accessed July 20, 2013).

Captain, Intelligence Section, Municipal Department in Central New York. 2013. Interview by author. Personal Interview. Tape Recorded. City in Central New York, August 6.

Deleuze, Gilles. 1992. "Postscript on Societies of Control" *October* 59 (Winter): 3–7.

Deputy Commissioner, New York Department of Criminal Justice Services, Office of Public Safety. 2013. Interview by author. Personal Interview. Tape Recorded. Albany, NY, June 13.

Detective, Nassau County Lead Development Center, County Police Department. 2013. Personal Interview. City in Long Island. August 13.

Detective Sergeant, County Sheriff. 2014. Interview by author. Phone Interview. Binghamton New York, June 12.

Director, Crime Analysis Center. 2013. Interview by author. Personal Interview. Tape Recorded. City in New York's Capital District. July 15.

Division of Criminal Justice Services. 2015. "Law Enforcement Personnel by Agency, Beginning 2007." Open NY Data Portal. https://data.ny.gov/Public-Safety/Law-Enforcement-Personnel-by-Agency-Beginning-2007/khn9-hhpq (Accessed March 15, 2016).

Division of Criminal Justice Services. 2009. "OPERATION IMPACT—Annual Report 2009." Division of Criminal Justice Services. http://www.criminaljustice.ny.gov/crimnet/ojsa/impact/2009annualreport.pdf (Accessed April 3, 2013).

Division of Criminal Justice Services. 2010. "OPERATION IMPACT—Annual Report 2010." Division of Criminal Justice Services. http://www.criminaljustice.ny.gov/crimnet/ojsa/impact/2010annualreport.pdf (Accessed April 3, 2013).

Division of Criminal Justice Services. 2011. "OPERATION IMPACT—Annual Report 2011." Division of Criminal Justice Services. http://www.criminaljustice.ny.gov/crimnet/ojsa/impact/2011annualreport.pdf (Accessed April 3, 2013).

Division of Criminal Justice Services. 2012. "OPERATION IMPACT—Annual Report 2012." Division of Criminal Justice Services. http://www.criminaljustice.ny.gov/crimnet/ojsa/impact/2012annualreport.pdf (Accessed April 3, 2013).

Division of Criminal Justice Services. 2013. "OPERATION IMPACT—Annual Report 2013." Division of Criminal Justice Services. http://www.criminaljustice.ny.gov/crimnet/ojsa/impact/2010annualreport.pdf (Accessed April 3, 2013).

Division of Criminal Justice Services. Director of Public Information. 2014. Email Message to Author. June 30.

Federal Bureau of Investigation. 2007. *Table 74—Full Time Police Employees*. Federal Bureau of Investigation. https://www2.fbi.gov/ucr/cius2007/data/table_74.html (Accessed December 15, 2014).

Federal Bureau of Investigation. 2013. *Table 74—Full Time Police Employees*. Federal Bureau of Investigation. https://www.fbi.gov/about-us/cjis/ucr/crime-in-the-u.s/2014/crime-in-the-u.s.-2014/tables/table-74 (Accessed March 15, 2016).

Feeley, Malcolm M. and Jonathan Simon. 1992. "The New Penology: Notes on the Emerging Strategy of Corrections and Its Implications." *Criminology* 30, no. 4 (November): 449–74.

Field Intelligence Officer. 2014. Interview by author. Phone Interview. Binghamton New York, June 3.

Foucault, Michel. 2009. *Security, Territory, Population: Lectures at the Collège de France 1977–1978*. New York: Macmillan.

Garland, David. 2012. *The Culture of Control: Crime and Social order in Contemporary Society*. Chicago: University of Chicago Press.

Garland, David. 1996. "The Limits of the Sovereign State Strategies of Crime Control in Contemporary Society." *British Journal of Criminology* 36, no. 4 (Autumn): 445–71.

Gilmore, Ruth. 2006. *Golden Gulag: Prisons, Surplus, Crisis, and Opposition in Globalizing California*. Berkeley: University of California Press.

Gottschalk, Marie. 2010. "Cell Blocks & Red Ink: Mass Incarceration, the Great Recession & Penal Reform." *Daedalus* 139, no. 3 (Summer): 62–73.

Haggerty, Kevin D. and Richard V. Ericson. 2000. "The Surveillant Assemblage." *The British Journal of Sociology* 51, no. 4 (December): 605–22.

Innes, Martin. 2006. "Policing Uncertainty: Countering Terror through Community Intelligence and Democratic Policing." *The Annals of the American Academy of Political and Social Science* 605, no. 1 (May): 222–41.

Innes, Martin, Laurence Abbott, Trudy Lowe, and Colin Roberts. 2009. "Seeing Like a Citizen: Field Experiments in 'Community Intelligence-led Policing'." *Police Practice and Research* 10, no. 2 (April): 99–114.

Kava, Janine. 2008. "Crime Fighting Efforts in Western New York Get a Boost." Division of Criminal Justice Services. Press Release, July 7. http://www.criminaljustice.ny.gov/pio/press_releases/2008-07-07a_pressrelease.html (April 3, 2013).

Kyckelhahn, Tracey. 2015a. "Justice Expenditure and Employment Extracts, 2009—Final." Bureau of Justice Statistics, July 1. http://www.bjs.gov/index.cfm?ty=pbdetail&iid=5048 (Accessed March 7, 2016).

Kyckelhahn, Tracey. 2015b. "Justice Expenditure and Employment Extracts, 2012—Preliminary." Bureau of Justice Statistics, February 26. http://www.bjs.gov/index.cfm?ty=pbdetail&iid=5239 (Accessed March 7, 2016).

Lucken, Karol. 1997. "Privatizing Discretion: 'Rehabilitating' Treatment in Community Corrections." *Crime & Delinquency* 43, no. 3 (July): 243–59.

Maguire, Mike and Tom John. 2006. "Intelligence-Led Policing, Managerialism and Community Engagement: Competing Priorities and the Role of the National Intelligence Model in the UK." *Policing & Society* 16, no. 1 (August): 67–85.

Manza, Jeff and Christopher Uggen. 2006. *Locked Out: Felon Disenfranchisement and American Democracy: Felon Disenfranchisement and American Democracy*. New York: Oxford University Press.

McQuade, Brendan. 2016. "Police and the Post-9/11 Surveillance Surge: 'Technological Dramas' in the 'Bureaucratic Field'." *Surveillance & Society* 14, no. 1: 1–19.

McQuade, Brendan. 2015a. "The Demilitarization Ruse." *Jacobin*, May 24. https://www.jacobinmag.com/2015/05/camden-obama-police-brutality-black-lives-matter/ (Accessed May 24 2015).

McQuade, Brendan. 2015b. "Against Community Policing." *Jacobin*, November 18. https://www.jacobinmag.com/2015/11/obama-chicago-black-lives-matter-police-brutality/ (Accessed November 18, 2015).

Miller, Reuben Jonathan. 2014. "Devolving the Carceral State: Race, Prisoner Reentry, and the Micro-Politics of Urban Poverty Management." *Punishment & Society* 16, no. 3 (July): 305–35.

Neocleous, Mark. 2000. *The Fabrication of Social Order: Critical Theory of Police Power*. London: Pluto Press.

Neocleous, Mark. 2014. *War Power, Police Power*. Edinburgh: Edinburgh University Press.

NY/NJ HIDTA Director/Former DCJS Director. 2013. Personal Interview. New York, NY. September 27.

O'Hara, Jim. 2008. "New Program Targets Chronic Criminals." *The Syracuse Post-Standard*, May 6. http://www.syracuse.com/news/index.ssf/2008/05/new_program_targets_chronic_cr.html (Accessed August 3, 2013).

O'Malley, Pat. 1999. "Volatile and Contradictory Punishment," *Theoretical Criminology* 40, no. 1 (January): 175–96.

Police Chief, City in New York's Capital Region. 2013. Interview by author. Phone Interview. Tape Recorded. Binghamton, NY. June 28.

Police Chief. 2013. Interview by author. Personal Interview. Tape Recorded. City in New York's Mid-Hudson Region. July 19.

Police Chief. 2013. Interview by author. Personal Interview. Tape Recorded. City in New York's Finger Lake Region. August 22.

Probation Officer. 2014. Interview by author. Personal Interview. Tape Recorded. City in New York's Mohawk Valley. May 13.

Raeff, Marc. 1983. *The Well-Ordered Police State: Social and Institutional Change Through Law in the Germanies and Russia, 1600–1800*. New Haven: Yale University Press.

Ratcliffe, Jerry. 2008. *Intelligence-led Policing*. Portland: Wilan Publishing.

Reaves, Brian. 2010. "Local Police Departments, 2007." Bureau of Justice Statistics, December. http://www.bjs.gov/content/pub/pdf/lpd07.pdf (Accessed March 7, 2016).

Reaves, Brian. 2015. "Local Police Departments, 2013." Bureau of Justice Statistics, May. http://www.bjs.gov/content/pub/pdf/lpd13ppp.pdf (Accessed March 7, 2016).

Rigakos, George S. and Richard W. Hadden. 2001. "'Crime, Capitalism and the Risk Society': Towards the Same Olde Modernity?" *Theoretical Criminology* 5, no. 1 (Feburary): 61–84.

Rose, Nikolas. 2000. "Government and Control." *British Journal of Criminology* 40, no. 3 (Spring): 321–39.

Silverman, Eli B. 1999. *NYPD Battles Crime: Innovative Strategies in Policing*. Boston: Northeastern University Press.

Wacquant, Loïc. 2009. *Punishing the Poor: The Neoliberal Government of Social Insecurity*. Durham: Duke University Press Books.

Walsh, William F. and Gennaro F. Vito. 2004. "The Meaning of Compstat Analysis and Response." *Journal of Contemporary Criminal Justice* 20, no. 1 (February): 51–69.

Zedner, Lucia. 2006. "Policing Before and After the Police: The Historical Antecedents of Contemporary Crime Control." *British Journal of Criminology* 46, no. 1 (January): 78–96.

Chapter 4

Serving Two Masters? Reentry Task Forces and Justice Disinvestment

Joshua M. Price

It is June, 2015, in Binghamton, New York.[1] I am in my living room with two people I'll call Jerry and Carol. Both have served time in jail and now they work for community-based organizations. I have known them for about ten years. Jerry listens attentively as Carol and I conduct an informal inquest into the county reentry task force. To call it an "inquest," however, is premature: the patient is not yet dead. But it is weak and may be dying. Jerry, Carol and I collaborated with others to found the task force about six years ago. They are bitterly disappointed with the direction it has taken. After about forty minutes, Jerry remarks that the task force has failed to advocate for the formerly incarcerated. To illustrate, he describes his effort to start a campaign to "Ban the Box," or ban questions about previous criminal convictions from employment forms as a way to facilitate employment of people with a criminal record.

> Ban the Box—that I'd talked to [the local reentry coordinator] about—he's just not interested in that because that requires canvassing the neighborhood and getting to know the neighborhood, and putting your neck out and giving your opinion on something. (fieldnotes 2015)

Jerry's example of the unwillingness of a local reentry task force coordinator to take on the "Ban the Box" campaign captures a tension at the heart of this chapter. No one can serve two masters. Yet this is precisely the dilemma that many reentry task forces, agencies, and organizations confront. Many promise to serve criminal justice goals to monitor, punish and assure public safety. Yet as Naomi Murakawa has shown, this emphasis on a right to public safety propelled the development of a racialized carceral state in the first place (Murakawa 2014, 3–4). It is not surprising, then, that the goals of keeping the formerly incarcerated under supervision and trying to prevent them from reoffending combine awkwardly with the larger aims of promoting the civil rights of the formerly incarcerated, advocating for criminal justice reform, and changing the social conditions that land people in prison in the first place. What unites these two tendencies is the objective of reintegrating people after incarceration so that they can lead healthy lives of civic participation. But this larger goal papers over deep divergences in the people it brings together.

The county-run task forces that one now finds throughout New York State are an example of how state authority has devolved to local control, engendering conflict and competition among actors in each county as they jockey for funds and power to oversee people who have just gotten out of prison. The professionalization and institutionalization of the task forces, moreover, has meant that reentry is less peer-oriented and more coercive than before; the shift signals a denial or reversal of participation by the formerly incarcerated (such as Jerry and Carol) at both a policy and a practical level. A related consequence has been a renewed focus on simply *managing* formerly incarcerated people, often aided by actuarial software. Certainly little effort is directed at larger structural issues such as racism, unemployment, or poverty, or changing overly punitive laws.

Analysis of a set of interviews with reentry coordinators and formerly incarcerated people throws into relief differences between official accounts of reentry and the social facts on the ground—the disparities between policy and practice. These interviews also uncover the contrast between what formerly incarcerated people want and what they get.[2] There is an auto-ethnographic part of this research as well; even though I have never been incarcerated, I have provided advocacy for the formerly incarcerated in formal and informal capacities and I participated in setting up our local task force. This has given me something like an insider's view of the task forces, even as I have tried here to provide as circumspect an analysis as I can.

In the latter half of this chapter, as a way to illustrate how the reentry task forces seek normative solutions that are internally inconsistent, I briefly examine different moral understandings of the formerly incarcerated person that are implicitly at work in the universe of reentry organizations.

THE GROWTH OF A REENTRY INDUSTRY, DISINVESTMENT, AND THE SHIFT TO THE LOCAL

As recently as 2010, Michael Tonry argued that, "In our time, broad-based agreement that prison populations should be radically reduced does not exist" (2010, 641). What a difference a day makes. By 2014, Republicans with libertarian tendencies have tentatively begun to join liberals in calling for reform. A broad consensus, it seems, is emerging to reduce prison rolls. Proposals include revising drug policy, abolishing mandatory minimums, and closing correctional facilities. In fact, the number of people incarcerated in the United States has declined almost 3 percent since 2008–2009, to around 1.54 million people (as of 2014), but still geometrically more than the 200,000 people incarcerated in 1972. The prison population in New York has decreased much more drastically since 1999 from nearly 73,000 in 1999 to just over 52,000 in 2015 (Beck and Harrison 2001, 3; Commission on Correction 2016).

One implication of the deflating balloon is that nationally the number of people who return to their communities each year is at record levels. In the last few years, an average of roughly 700,000 people—in New York over 25,000 people—return home each year from prison (Guerino, Harrison, and Sobol 2012). The magnitude of people returning has engendered a complex set of responses from state and non-state actors. Private interests, public interests, political ambitions, state agencies, and the nonprofit sector are rearticulating their relationships. This has meant a slow expansion, or possibly transition, from mass incarceration to mass supervision (Robinson, McNeill, and Maruna 2013; McNeill and Beyens 2014; Miller 2014; Price 2015, 147). Governmental and nongovernmental organizations compete to administer to the formerly incarcerated and their families.

What are the consequences of this shift? We can take as our point of departure Reuben Miller's (2014) account of carceral devolution as "a set of interrelated policies that transfer carceral authority—in this case the authority to rehabilitate and supervise prisoners—from federal and state-based institutions to local ones."

> Geographically, rehabilitation has been outsourced and privatized, moving from within prison walls and into the therapeutic spaces, church basements, and community centers of the inner city. Conceptually, reentry service providers seek to "change prisoners' lives," transforming them into "productive citizens"—rational, self-sufficient actors who demonstrate a willingness to seek out pro-social relationships, work the most available and immediate jobs, and submit to a lifelong process of introspection, re-evaluation, and change. The ascendance of prisoner reentry, as the rehabilitative strategy of choice in the current age, is among the most visible features of Carceral Devolution. (2014, 308)

In another article, however, published at about the same time, Austin, Cadora, Clear, et al. argue that the eighteen states experimenting with "justice reinvestment" have largely overlooked local actors.[3] "By focusing on state-level political and administrative policymakers, the JRI [justice reinvestment initiative] process has too often marginalized well-established local advocates and justice reformers who bring knowledge of local conditions and politics to the table, and who have a vested interest in providing long-term implementation oversight and ensuring sustainability of reforms" (2013, 2).

New York's dominant reentry strategies reflect both trends—devolution to nonprofits and local actors who seek to change offenders into "productive citizens," as well as deference to state-level, top-down initiatives. Government agencies such as parole, corrections, and the Department of Social Services (DSS) continue to play a large role. These reentry task forces, however, tend to overlook or leave out *some* local actors, including many who had been most involved in local advocacy: anti-racist grass roots organizations, civil rights leaders, prominent activists and mentors who have been to prison, and other community leaders and social justice advocates who often played a key role in providing whatever support there had been in upstate New York before the advent of the task forces.

NEW YORK STATE AND THE ROLE OF PAROLE

Let's take Binghamton as a typical example of how these task forces work. Binghamton is an upstate, deindustrialized rust-belt city with high unemployment rates. At one time in the recent past, before the task forces, one was met with little by way of support on coming back into town after serving time in the penitentiary. No formal process existed outside of meeting with one's parole officer (and about 80 percent of people who come out are initially on parole). Reentry was not organized. What little could be found consisted of a hodgepodge of religious charities, service organizations, homeless advocates, twelve-step programs, a day labor organization and a few key people, many themselves formerly incarcerated, who helped out, and whom one could learn of and contact through a local grapevine. These groups and individuals assisted to a greater or lesser degree in aiding a person in obtaining affordable housing, furniture and groceries, clothes, employment and employment training, health care, substance abuse counseling, and so on. The relationships among the actors were informal. One navigated through these systems as best one could. Whether one's parole officer was helpful depended on the luck of the draw, and more often than not the parole officer placed law enforcement before social service. A man reflected on his experiences before the task force was set up.

> When I came home [from prison], there was no parole [that offered any help], no reentry, nothing set up. I was scrapping and asking and looking. That's why I contacted you. . . .[4] There was nothing. They had the Council of Churches and they didn't have any money. They were more geared towards guys getting out

> of county jail with a little something to get you through the night—packages and stuff like that. I was looking more for work with employment, maybe training, just to see what was available. (fieldnotes 2015)

What role did the parole office play in bread-and-butter issues such as finding a job?

> *Q:* Did parole help you figure out how to get a job, job training, or anything like that?
>
> *A:* No, no, no, no. They don't offer any of that. They just tell you where they *don't* want you to work if they don't want you to be near something or don't want you to do this. Because my crime involved stealing, I was not to get a job in retail where I would handle money. You are not to do that. It's not up to the employer to decide, it's up to them. And they wanted money from me. As soon as I got employed they wanted their $30 a month. And there's no guidance, no help. Every once on a while you'd hear an officer say, "I hear over at such and such they're hiring."
>
> *Q:* Did they put pressure on you to get a job?
>
> *A:* Oh, yeah. Yeah. The tension eased once you got a job. They seemed content. You're looking good on their roll.

Most people I interviewed reflected this attitude. At best, parole officers neither aided nor hindered. At worst, parole officers have gone so far as to undermine people on parole (Paley and Price 2010; Price 2015). Further examples came out in interviews I conducted in 2015. "They're allowed to give you money. They're allowed to give you—I forget the name of it, pocket money, cash door money. If someone's not doing too well, rather than see him risk his freedom, we can help him. But there's never any of that assistance." Generally speaking, "They didn't do anything, they didn't guide you." Parole officers did exhort people on parole to find employment quickly. It did not make any difference that finding employment was particularly difficult with a criminal record and even more difficult in the face of larger, structural problems in the society, such as widespread unemployment after the 2008 recession. One man who was released at that time noted how unsympathetic the parole office was to his plight.

> *Q:* I remember you came out at a time of record unemployment. Remember that?
>
> *A:* And parole here was just awful. It was the worst thing I'd ever encountered. You can rant and rave all you want but until you've experienced that. . . . (fieldnotes 2015)

It is important to understand the role of the parole office since they are basic to the functioning of the task forces. Parole officers exercise enormous control over the lives of people on parole and the vast majority of people released from prison are released on parole. Parole officers have the power to mandate programs and services the person on parole must take, such as anger-management or drug programs. Parole can also dictate where a person may work, live, set a curfew, and establish other conditions of daily life. The parole office can—and often does—require that a person live away from family or even a spouse if they determine that this would facilitate a successful reentry (where success means that the person will not reoffend).

RISE OF REENTRY TASK FORCES, SURVEILLANT ASSEMBLAGES, AND PYRRHIC DEFEAT

In what will serve as a signal event for this chapter, in 2005 New York State established an initiative to fund county-level reentry task forces. Counties across New York State began to form reentry task forces. Each interested county created commissions with designated chairs and staff drawn from county government. With the support of the county executive, each commission or task force could apply for grants of up to $100,000 to hire a reentry coordinator who would act at the behest of the task force. Typically, the task forces include representatives from probation, the district attorney's office, Department of Corrections and Community Supervision (which includes parole), law enforcement, DSS, AIDS advocacy organizations, officials from public housing, religious institutions, drug treatment organizations, and other nonprofits.

The call for proposals at the state level resulted initially in promoting competition among agencies and organizations that, if not intentional, certainly could have been foreseen. In order to receive state funds, the state required that organizations work together to form comprehensive task forces, even as the state funneled funds through only *one* organization to spearhead the efforts. The state's financial incentive thus simultaneously engendered conflict as local organizations elbowed for a place at the trough, even as they had to work together (or appear to work together) to form the task force as a condition for eligibility.

Some organizations, especially DSS and the office of parole, had a stronger hand in this process and thus typically retained primacy. This led to a second, related consequence of the devolution of power and management. The agencies or organizations that received the state funding shunted aside formerly incarcerated persons and activists, who in some locations had led the campaign for reentry services in the first place. In at least two counties, the parole office or DSS has cited confidentiality requirements to exclude the formerly incarcerated and their families from serving on the task forces, on the pretext that specific case files may be discussed in task force meetings. These new and newly enhanced relationships of formal interagency collaboration, in other words, incorporate some existing grassroots organizations and networks, while marginalizing others, and devolve power and decision making to the most established municipal, county, and regional actors, whether the leaders of prominent nonprofit organizations or administrators in local government agencies.

This was the case in Broome County, where Binghamton is located. An association of formerly incarcerated people and their allies initiated the task force. This group operated according to peer-models of counseling and education, and made decisions by consensus and according to a principle of horizontal, non-hierarchal decision making (Sitrin 2006). Yet once the DSS and the office of parole got involved, most of the formerly incarcerated people and their family members lost any real authority they had in the task force, and in one case (a registered sex offender), was explicitly forbidden from attending any meetings.

As of 2015, eighteen counties have formed task forces. In a time of shrinking budgets, to whom are they beholden? What form of "reentry" and "reform" do they produce, and to whose benefit? Some years ago, Haggerty and Erickson characterized an emergent "surveillant assemblage" to analyze the convergence of once discrete surveillance systems (2000; 606). Though the notion of a "surveillant assemblage" is helpful analytically, new trends seem to indicate that the relationships and coordination are neither functional nor coherent, and in fact often fail to achieve their objectives (see Ferguson 1994, 8).

People returning from prison meet an array of organizations that have conflicting priorities, goals, and even different concepts of responsibility. Parole, DSS, and centers for workplace training, homeless shelters, housing agencies, outpatient psychiatric services, schools, employment programs, child protective services, and drug rehabilitation clinics all have different, if overlapping, points of intervention. As parole officers often require people on parole to attend other programs, these programs also come to wield a degree of power and control. This byzantine structure of reentry serves an unspoken, and possibly unintended, management function. Because of the flattening and spread of actors through reentry process, no one is responsible for failure (however failure is measured), except the returning former "offender" himself or herself.[5] Different forms of social control end up placing responsibility for rehabilitative self-governance on the individual (I return to this theme in the latter half of the chapter).

Conversely, this social arrangement relieves the programs and agencies of some of their responsibility. Indeed, failure to integrate a person back into the community after incarceration arguably yields *benefits* to those organizations involved and does not involve any direct costs to those organizations, a set up that Paul Reiman might term a "Pyrrhic defeat" (Reiman 2012, 1). Generally speaking, agencies and organizations are not themselves sanctioned or punished if they sanction or punish the formerly incarcerated (impose fines, remand a person to custody, suspend benefits, remove children, and so on). But if a high number of people fail to reintegrate successfully, then as a matter of public policy, the aggregate failure serves as a justification for greater funding for reentry in general (and hence for reentry organizations) so that people can reintegrate successfully in the future.

Because each task force developed independently, they exhibit some diversity in composition and orientation, despite some commonalities. Some task forces see reentry as a criminal justice issue related to monitoring high-risk offenders and others as a question of providing a proper net of social services. Some task forces are housed within a district attorney's office, while others are aligned more closely with DSS, or are organized, supported, and controlled primarily by the nonprofit sector. One task force coordinator told us that he works with the district attorney's office, the commissioner of mental health, the sheriff's department, the local police, the social security administration, a coalition of local churches and thirty-four other agencies (fieldnotes 2015).

Only one reentry task force coordinator (from a major metropolitan center in downstate New York) characterized the issue of reentry as a "civil rights" issue. "These individuals have the right to services of post incarceration," she reasoned. "As a result of the war on drugs, we have a moral responsibility to make sure these services are provided in transitioning back. . . ." (fieldnotes October, 2015).

But her view is in the minority. Most reentry task force coordinators, and most task forces, subject the person to a process of individualizing what might be otherwise viewed as a collective civil rights issue. At the same time, the person is subject to expanding processes of social control. This is consistent with the state's overall goals. According to the New York Division of Criminal Justice Services (DCJS), the goals of the reentry task force initiative include:

a. Identify gaps in services that are required to reduce the risk of reoffending.
b. Identify barriers to accessing available services to reduce the risk of reoffending.

For its part, case management should:

c. Work with local parole to target individuals returning to the community who present high risk of reoffending.
d. Assess needs related to reoffending (Offender Reentry Task Force Initiative n.d.)

Note that all of these goals have reducing the risk of reoffending as their objective. By emphasizing the risk of reoffending over advocacy, the task forces tend to individualize social problems (poverty, racism, the stigma of serving time in prison, housing discrimination, gender-based inequity, and so on) and reduce successful reentry simply to a question of not committing future criminal acts. To the extent that task forces encourage or even allow people to congregate in groups, for example, it is for therapeutic purposes, such as anger-management. Indeed, because the parole office does not allow fraternization among formerly incarcerated, the parole office sanctions group assembly. In this way, collective advocacy or movement building is undermined, and in fact actively discouraged.

Due to all these factors, and due also in part to their institutional and financial dependence on state agencies and their dependence on the authority of the parole office, task forces generally do not attempt any structural or institutional changes in their local communities, let alone the larger society; the only exception is that they seek better coordination and flow of information between programs and services. But this is consistent with the twin goals of monitoring their clients effectively and getting them to adapt to their restricted circumstances.

In many ways, the task forces consolidate existing formal and informal mechanisms of tracking, containing, and partially incapacitating the formerly incarcerated so that the freedom of the free world is, for them, increasingly impoverished. As the state retreats administratively, a surveillance net thus extends itself not only over their lives, but also over their families (Price 2015). In this sense, at least, a surveillant assemblage seems to have been put in place. They are targeted for regulatory social service and criminal justice interventions (see Miller 2014).

TASK FORCES VIEWED FROM BELOW

The result is plain enough to the formerly incarcerated. One man told me his expectations of a community reentry program.

> [When] reentry was designed, you thought "All right, they're going to get you interviews, give you a nice list of people who need, who will hire felons, get you with a resume." (fieldnotes 2015)

But he was disappointed to find that he received no help. One person who had served several decades in prison remarked upon the influence of parole on the culture of reentry. At an orientation he attended, the reentry coordinator, a civilian hired to aid in reentry:

> gave a spiel, and he sounded like a representative from parole. He was telling them, "Look, if you are going to be in this reentry, you *have* to come. Your parole officer will be notified if you don't. You *have* to take these programs. If you're going to be in my program, you have to take these programs. And if you don't your parole officer will be notified." So it didn't sound like reentry to me. It sounded like an offshoot of parole. And that's just what the guys [the men and women just released from prison] . . . they don't want more parole. They want less. I was hearing a lot of people tell me they didn't want the reentry. And this kid I was talking to he was telling me he didn't want the reentry. "I don't need it, I'll get my own job. I'm fine." It definitely created a sense of . . . I don't really know what they're doing for them. (fieldnotes 2015)

People coming back from prison, this man was at pains to point out, "want reentry programs," so it is not that they do not want assistance, "but they don't want to deal with this." Speaking of the reentry coordinator, "He came across like he's one of the parole officers and you're going to do this and you're going to do that." The man concluded, "And I was taken aback by that." Then he asked me, "Is reentry funded by parole?" In fact, I told him, the New York State Department of Criminal Justice Services funds the reentry program through the county, but this man's intuition that parole is behind it betrays his sense of the outsize role they play in some counties in administering reentry task forces.

Through the task forces, state agencies' day-to-day decision-making is delegated to the local and regional level, while allowing the state to set broad policy goals. However, the power of these vertical relationships can be overstated. New policies imposed from above are not always applied in a timely or consistent way by rank-and-file officers or staff (see Lynch 1998). Reentry coordinators who are charged with offering employment services, but instead "sound like a representative from parole," is but one example.

The interviews I conducted with formerly incarcerated people demonstrated that they saw a consistent distinction between what they wanted or needed and what the task force provided. A formerly incarcerated man who had observed a task force coordinator at some length thought the task force coordinator delegated or "dispatched" authority in the key area of employment referral.

> *A:* And all he really does is dispatch people to other people. He dispatches them. It's all I ever see him do.
>
> *Q:* What do you mean?
>
> *A:* Dispatches them. Like [for example, he would say], "Ok, you go see this girl at this place for the Department of Labor." "You go see this girl at this place for this and that."

> *Q:* Oh, the people he's supposed to be working with. What would you like to see him do?
>
> *A:* I don't know. I always thought reentry would be like you walk in and it would be something where they could take care of you right there. There was never. . . . There wasn't no employment specialist. For parole. I don't need to go to Department of Labor. I can go there on my own. I needed someone who was aware, had relations with employers that take felons: "Here's what we want, you send us these people, we'll work with you." We wanted people who could get parolees apartments.
>
> *Q:* You mean a one-stop shop?
>
> A: Yeah, and he really doesn't do that. He distributes it . . . I don't think he employs experts and he just shingles it out. (fieldnotes 2015)

Most formerly incarcerated people were under no illusions that the reentry task force had their best interest in mind or was answerable to their needs. One formerly incarcerated woman commented to me,

> It's pretty obvious that they didn't want someone who was going to advocate or that understood the population. And it was pretty obvious that they had no real intention of helping the population. That was never the intent. The intent was to get the money, get the criminal justice division off their back. They didn't want anyone who really was going to advocate for the population, they just wanted somebody who was going to do what the powers-that-be wanted them to do. (fieldnotes 2015)

This woman, who had played a key role in starting the task force, saw the task force as now focused on fulfilling the requirements of state funders and in this sense absorbed with self-perpetuating rather than on taking seriously the experiences of the incarcerated and their concerns. This is why she and others we interviewed favored a peer-model. "The peer piece is crucial," another person told me. The people who run reentry "should reflect the population that has been let out." Reentry personnel should be other formerly incarcerated people. A formerly incarcerated man who had been involved in starting a task force in his county argued that the failures (from his perspective) of his county task force rested with the structure of the funding and the way funding is funneled through certain agencies or entities:

> When you're going after grants like that, you really have to look at who you're giving the grant over to. The grant would really have been a great grant if we could have turned it over to the right entity. And we had to look at who really has the power to decide how it would have been administered. . . . Parole . . . [has] the power. (fieldnotes 2015)

The parole office serves as a gatekeeper and retains veto power over many initiatives since their cooperation is necessary for most initiatives to survive. For example, several people I interviewed argued that involvement by the parole office ruled out any possible peer-model for reentry. One woman gave me an example. The parole office "blocked me from being hired [to a reentry job on the task force] because I was married to a person on parole." She observed that this had to do less with her qualifications (she had already been hired) than with how parole held at arm's length the incarcerated and their families, whom the task forces were, after all, set up to support. She thought stigma played a role. "At the time they turned the formerly incarcerated population into this predatory, sex-offender population." She was tarred by the same feather. A formerly incarcerated man, referring to the incident,

> The outcome would have been different with D. in there, but the reality is that it would have only been different because D. would have been willing to push the envelope. And found a way to do it. [The current coordinator] has been unwilling to do that. Job security has been his main thing. Not doing for the formerly incarcerated. The reality is that those who are on parole, which is the only ones this grant covers, are a small number compared to the overall formerly incarcerated. What you should be doing is trying to develop programs that benefit the largest group of individuals, not just your little specific group. (fieldnotes 2015)

He thought that commitment to the larger group of formerly incarcerated people is now off the table. D. mused ruefully on how she might have contributed if she had not been disqualified from participating.

> I would have advocated. I already had a really good understanding of that system, and [the current coordinator] doesn't. He is new to this community. He doesn't understand the culture and the history as I did. And I know a lot of the agencies because I used them. What worked, what didn't and what the criteria is. If someone were to ask me about something, I'd say, well, that's a waste of time, but what if we tried this instead. [The current coordinator] may have gotten there but it's not an immediate thing. (fieldnotes 2015)

She thought someone who had used the services as a client was at an advantage. Not all formerly incarcerated people agreed that the model had to be peer-to-peer.

> *Q:* Do you think it's important that the person who does that job is formerly incarcerated? That it's a peer thing? Or you don't necessarily think it's important?
>
> *A:* I don't know. No, it wouldn't matter.
>
> *Q:* For some people it's important. . . .

> *A:* If the person is doing an outstanding job and a legitimate job. You can't always trust an ex-con. It's nice to show you got a few working with you, side by side. And you're getting results. I speak about stopping abuse, I believe in stopping it. I have buddies back inside the system. I went through it. No one cares about the prisoner. (fieldnotes 2015)

This man suggests that while a peer component is crucial to some, and while it is important to show that reentry organizations practice what they preach by hiring the formerly incarcerated, what is most important is that a coordinator is competent at "getting results." As a formerly incarcerated man, his commitment is deep and deeply personal. But expertise must go beyond that.

> *Q:* What would you like . . . ? What you would like reentry to look like . . . ?
>
> *A:* Someone who's expert . . . who wants to deal with us. If I'm coming home and I am sitting in an employment office. And he says, "Ok, let's get your resume going. . . . These places will deal with you, these people won't." (fieldnotes 2015)

Not all blame can be laid at the door of the office of parole. The DSS also sets a number of rules and guidelines and fulfills a monitoring function. In fact, nothing symbolizes the allegiances and complex agenda of the task force as much as the "forty-five day" rule DSS imposes. Applicants for social services in New York must wait forty-five days for benefits, with the exception of a few stopgap emergency benefits that might be available (Temporary Assistance Source Book/New York State Office of Temporary and Disability Assistance 2011).

In many New York counties, DSS will not allow incarcerated people to apply from prison or jail, even if they are about to be released. This means that they will have to wait the full forty-five days once they are released. During this waiting period, formerly incarcerated people are in a particularly vulnerable situation. The irony of this is not lost on the formerly incarcerated. As one woman commented in an interview, "And if you go to the Welfare, you know you got to be waiting forty-five days. That's just like telling them to go back out there and do what they got to do. Steal, sell drugs or whatever" (Interview with a formerly incarcerated woman in Price 2015, 115). Activists, advocates, and even some reentry coordinators cited this forty-five day rule as a significant barrier to successful reentry.

> Ibrahim [who had served ten years in prison] . . . says we need to work to change the social services rule that requires a forty-five-day wait period to get social service benefits after one applies, because that's a hardship for people who come back from incarceration. "What are they supposed to do during those forty-five days?" (Price 2015, 139)

Over the course of more than a decade in Broome County, community organizations have repeatedly called for a change in policy to allow people to apply for DSS assistance programs while incarcerated so that benefits await them on their release. Even after more than a year at the helm of the reentry task force in Broome County, the DSS commissioner had still not changed his policy, but this could not be because he did not know the burden it imposed on people when they are first let out of prison (or the corresponding public safety risk when people are desperate and have basic needs that are unfulfilled). Indeed, in a meeting between the director of DSS and a group of local advocates for the formerly incarcerated, he dismissed repeated requests that he rescind, or even justify, the policy. The continued prevalence of the forty-five day rule represents the Janus-faced nature of DSS. On the one hand, throughout New York, representatives from DSS sit on the task force. They would thus be aware that continuity of services is one of the chief challenges facing the formerly incarcerated when they reenter the community. Yet on the other hand they continue policies with dubious bureaucratic justification that pose a significant barrier for successful reentry, even as they insert themselves into task forces that mold reentry throughout the state.

RISK ASSESSMENT VS. THE MORAL AGENT: WARRING CONCEPTS OF THE INDIVIDUAL

I argued above that the task forces tend to individualize social problems. Most social service agencies and the criminal justice system do so as well. What does this mean? And what understanding or model of "the individual" do they use? To clarify the inconsistent and conflicted mission of the task forces, let's follow an individual subject who goes through the reentry task force. As we follow, we can see how the use of risk-assessment software runs at odds with the concept of culpability that the criminal justice system generally uses as well as contradicting the commitment to self-improvement and self-betterment on which many of the social service and drug treatment programs rely.

For most people in state prison, the first stop in the reentry process is the parole board. By statute, the parole board receives a risk assessment of each person who goes before them (Rethinking Reentry 2012). The risk assessment is based on a questionnaire. The questions are designed to elicit information that can be used to calculate the risk the person will recidivate. The answers are entered as data into a computer software program known as COMPAS (Correctional Offender Management Profiling for Alternative Sanction). The COMPAS program yields information on risk levels that the parole board takes into consideration along with a variety of other factors as it decides whether to grant a person parole. New York has spent about $850 thousand dollars for this actuarial software (Open Book New York 2014). According to the New York State Office of Probation and Correctional Alternatives (OPCA) that mandates the use of the software:

> COMPAS is a standardized risk and needs assessment tool covering four different types of risk (violence, recidivism, failure to appear in court, and community non-compliance), and 18 different criminogenic needs. The software also includes case planning and reports generation features. (Aldi 2012)

Applying actuarial software—a set of risk factors—to establish the risk someone poses disaggregates the human subject into a set of data points that then flow through a series of administrative offices (see Haggerty and Erickson 2000, 608–09).

These data points are consequential for that human subject because of their weight in parole decision-making. The COMPAS program has altered reentry—not just whether a person will be paroled, but also to "determine how intensively parolees will be supervised . . . (Aldi 2012)." Once a person is paroled and she reaches the community to which she is paroled (which is usually the county where she received her original charge), the local parole office and the reentry coordinator also receive this COMPAS risk-assessment. This tool may be used at the discretion of the task forces, leading to inconsistent use. One task force coordinator communicated a sense of how it is used in an email:

> It is useful to gather some information (self-reporting leaves some doubt) like if crimes were committed while under the influence. It can show if the person has some insight. (fieldnotes 2015)

This coordinator implied that while important, it was not determinative: "We can use it as part of a psycho-social assessment."

One of the selling points of actuarial software is that it removes bias. However, the previous arrest record, a standard data point for COMPAS, can be a proxy for race, as Bernard Harcourt has argued (cited in Walker 2013). Since the criminal justice system involves a racialized "winnowing" out of white people at each stage (arrest, laying of charges, indictment, conviction, prison sentence), African-Americans, Native Americans, Latinos and other people of color may have a longer rap sheet than their white peers for the same offenses (Reiman 2012, 8). Thus, facially neutral measures for factoring the likelihood of recidivism, which are important for determining whether a person will receive parole and at what level s/he will be supervised or monitored, in fact disfavor people from communities of color.

COMPAS is not the only risk-assessment tool used in reentry. In 2011, new guidelines for the reentry task forces from the DCJS required the use of "evidence-based practices." State contracts with the task forces now include performance-based outcomes, including cognitive behavioral interventions and employment-focused achievements measured by the attainment of specific goals (NYDCJS 2014). The key vocabulary is "evidence-based," "best-practices," "cost/benefit analyses." These speak to an empirically based approach to analysis of human action within a statistically based, probabilistic understanding of future behavior. Task force charters and mission statements are replete with, on the one hand, criminological vocabulary ("recidivism," "criminogenic," and so on) and on the other, the language of therapeutic modalities, including social work, self-help and twelve-step programs. The stated goal is to save money and reduce recidivism. Nevertheless, the performance-based goals may not speak to overall employment success, say, so much as "employability" as Miller terms it. What this means, in effect, is that people on parole may be required as a condition of their parole to go through job training. Performance is measured by successful graduation rates rather than eventual employment. Using graduation rate rather than employment rate as a measure can change rather significantly whether a particular program looks successful, particularly in an environment, and in a sector of the economy where the unemployment rate is quite high, even in the best of economic circumstances. Job training, anger-management, and other routine, mandated aspects of post-incarceration life for many on parole come to have an almost ritualistic or ceremonial role rather than a practical function (see Wacquant 2010; Miller 2014).

Using probability to predict future criminal acts and to assess overall individual fitness for parole contradicts on some level holding individuals accountable as moral agents (see Hacking 1991; Feeley and Simon 1992, 452–53). Risk-assessment tools such as COMPAS predict the likelihood that a person will recidivate based on relevant demographic information (age, criminal record, and so on). Risk-assessment implies or presupposes a set of laws of chance and probability, theories of behavior, and instrumentation for measurement and prediction, including such standard sociological practices as looking for and noting correlations, finding relationships among factors through multiple regression, and so on (Price 2008; Hacking 1990; Simon 1988; see also Ericson and Haggerty 1997; Haggerty 2001; Hawkins and Catalano 1993; Loeber and Farrington 1998). But this stands in tension with viewing people as possessing free will and full moral agency, fully responsible for their actions, including being legally responsible. And parole boards and parole officers also presuppose individual moral agency in deciding parole: display of moral reflection, an expression of remorse and a stated desire to change are valued (see Price 2015, 156–58). This is a contradiction at the heart of parole and the reentry process.

Each of these two logics (actuarial and individual moral agency) is in conflict with another logic that drives sentencing, parole, and reentry policy: a reliance on what could be termed (to use old-fashioned terms) individual gumption and moxie. According to the logic of gumption and moxie, which is akin to but distinct from the logic of moral agency, a person can reenter successfully if s/he has enough inner commitment and desire to succeed, consistent with a long-standing regnant ideology. Miller (2014) terms this "moral regeneration" and attributes to it organizational attempts to inculcate trustworthiness, tenacity, and dependability (318). "Our goal is to make them self-sufficient and more marketable. . . . [But] at the end of the day you've got to go out there. At the end of the day, it's on you," as one of Miller's informants put it (318). (It is with this logic, by the way, that in the day-to-day drudgery of meetings with one's parole officer, parole officers usually insist that people find steady employment, in the face of the challenges in a labor market that tends not to hire people with a felony conviction).

The logic of gumption is linked to what Katzenstein, et al., have called the trope of the "rehabilitated felon" or the "felon made good" (2010). They note among advocates the pervasive use of this figure of the meritorious ex-felon (as Alec Ewald terms it), who has now transitioned from being a parasite and a criminal to become a productive member of the community. This imagery of the once-bad-now rehabilitated felon, "appears in court cases, legislative hearings, and frequently in testimonies" (Katzenstein, et al. 2010, 1041–43; Ewald 2002). Public advocates deploy this language and imagery to try and show that criminals are capable of reform. In the reentry field, the trope can be used to demonstrate the need, and the effectiveness, of institutional intervention at the point of reentry to make sure that people returning to the community are helped to stay on the straight-and-narrow. This concept of the individual is different from the concept of the moral agent because it sees people in terms of potential, but also, crucially, in need of support to make the right decisions and to succeed (where success is measured in normative terms). The moral agent, on the other hand, is presupposed to be a fully autonomous individual unencumbered by history or by effective obstacles to right action. The moral agent, even if he or she is subject to systematic discrimination, in active addiction, or mentally ill, is obliged to fulfill his or her obligations and to act within the law.

CONCLUSION

The new reentry programs represent not only devolution, but also (with significant exceptions) a retreat from a campaign for social justice for those escaping the prison warehouse. One finds a greater degree of institutional control as more agencies are brought in or coordinated by the state. This has translated into a more authoritarian reentry regime of control, coercion, and surveillance. This overall tendency is what we have been calling justice disinvestment.

At the individual level, ideologies of self-help compete with actuarial systems to set supervisory levels (Lynch 1998; Price 2008). Governmental and nongovernmental organizations joust for local administrative power and control, even if their interests converge at certain points.

This is potentially a different sense of "decarceration" from those who see decarceration entirely in emancipatory terms. This is because this sense of decarceration involves the advance of new means of monitoring the poor and unruly, as well as the creation of new programs for social and psychosocial regulation.

Even as the prison population has dipped then, the outcome has involved a reformed reentry system that produces more tracking of people outside the prison and less liberty, more monitoring and less assistance, more obligations and fewer rights for the formerly incarcerated. Incarcerated people, their families and friends, and communities have often been excluded from participation in formal reentry work (López 2014).

The prospect of justice disinvestment, on the basis of what I have described above, is not simply the replacement of mass incarceration with enhanced, mass supervision. At its most stark, this process of state retreat and retraction could be framed as social abandonment of a vulnerable population (Fineman 2008). In this reading, having endowed a group that is already disproportionately poor and of color with the "negative credential" of a criminal record (Pager 2007), the state has left the formerly incarcerated to their fate.

An alternative, unrealized future would have drawn more on the collective wisdom of the formerly incarcerated to integrate their peers into the community after incarceration. In the best of worlds, this would be salubrious for everyone—the greater community, the families, and the formerly incarcerated themselves.

NOTES

1. This chapter draws in part on research conducted by Karen Mixson. I would like to thank her and Bill Martin, as well as Brendan McQuade, Andrew Pragacz, John Eason, Chungse Jung, Luis González, Kevin Revier, and Reuben J. Miller for their crucial comments and suggestions.

2. The research was qualitative. We conducted a phone survey of New York task force coordinators in spring, 2015. Each open-ended, in-depth interview lasted about forty-five minutes. The author took part in the formation of a Reentry Task Force in Broome County for which he went to numerous (even innumerable) meetings, and

had discussions with formerly incarcerated people and social service providers from roughly 2007 to 2012. For the current research, the author conducted an additional series of interviews in June and July of 2015 with formerly incarcerated people.

3. While New York has not opted for justice reinvestment overall, it has adopted some elements of this approach, as I argue below.

4. The author worked in a volunteer capacity to support formerly incarcerated people.

5. I thank Brendan McQuade and Andy Pragacz for this thought.

REFERENCES

Aldi, Nicole A., ed. 2012. "e-Focus." *New York State Office of Probation and Correctional Alternatives*. 111, December 17. http://www.criminaljustice.ny.gov/opca/efocus/efocus111.htm. Accessed June 25, 2016

Austin, James, Eric Cadora, Todd R. Clear, et al. 2013. "Ending Mass Incarceration: Charting a New Justice Reinvestment." *The Sentencing Project*. http://sentencingproject.org/wp-content/uploads/2015/12/Ending-Mass-Incarceration-Charting-a-New-Justice-Reinvestment.pdf. Accessed June 26, 2016.

Beck, By Allen J. and Paige M. Harrison. 2001. "Prisoners in 2000." NCJ 188207. Washington, DC: U.S. Department of Justice, Bureau of Justice Statistics, http://bjs.ojp.usdoj.gov/content/pub/pdf/p00.pdf. Accessed June 26, 2016.

Commission of Correction. 2016. "Inmate Population Statistics." http://www.scoc.ny.gov/pop.htm. Accessed April 1, 2016.

Ericson, Richard V. and Kevin D. 1997. *Policing the Risk Society*. Toronto: University of Toronto Press.

Ewald, Alec. 2002. "'Civil Death': The Ideological Paradox of Criminal Disenfranchisement Laws in the United States." *Wisconsin Law Review* 5 (1): 1045–137.

Feeley, Malcolm M. and Jonathan Simon. November 1992. "The New Penology: Notes on the Emerging Strategy of Corrections and Its Implications." *Criminology* 30 (4): 449–74.

Ferguson, James. 1994. *Anti-Politics Machine: Development, Depoliticization, and Bureaucratic Power in Lesotho*. Minneapolis, MN: University of Minnesota Press.

Fineman, Martha Albertson. 2008. "The Vulnerable Subject: Anchoring Equality in the Human Condition." *Yale Journal of Law and Feminism* 20 (1): 1–23.

Guerino, Paul, Paige Harrison, and William Sabol. 2012. "Prisoners in 2010." NCJ 236096. Washington, DC: U.S. Department of Justice, Bureau of Justice Statistics, http://www.bjs.gov/content/pub/pdf/p10.pdf. Accessed June 26, 2016.

Hacking, Ian I. 1990. *The Taming of Chance*. Cambridge, UK: Cambridge University Press.

Haggerty, Kevin D. 2001. *Making Crime Count*. Toronto: University of Toronto Press.

Haggerty, Kevin D. and Richard V. Ericson. December 2000. "The Surveillant Assemblage." *British Journal of Sociology* 51 (4): 605–22.

Hawkins, D. and Catalano, R. 1993. *Communities that Care: Risk-focused Prevention Using the Social Development Strategy*. Seattle, WA: Development Research and Programs, Inc.

Katzenstein, Mary Fainsod, Leila Mohsen Ibrahim, and Katherine D. Rubin. December 2010. "The Dark Side of American Liberalism and Felony Disenfranchisement." *Perspectives on Politics* 8 (4): 1035–54.

Loeber, R. and Farrington, D. P. 1998. *Serious and Violent Juvenile Offenders: Risk Factors and Successful Interventions.* Thousand Oaks, CA: Sage Publications.

López, Gerald P. 2014. "How Mainstream Reformers Design Ambitious Reentry Programs Doomed to Fail and Destined to Reinforce Targeted Mass Incarceration and Social Control." *Hastings Race and Poverty Law Journal* (Winter): 1–109.

Lynch, M. 1998. "Waste Managers? The New Penology, Crime Fighting, and Parole Agent Identity." *Law and Society Review* 32: 839–69.

McNeill, Fergus and Kristel Beyens. 2014. Introduction to *Offender Supervision in Europe*, edited by Fergus McNeill and Kristel Beyens. New York: Palgrave Macmillan.

Murakawa, Naomi. 2014. *The First Civil Right: How Liberals Built Prison America.* Oxford: Oxford University Press.

NYDCJS. 2014. New York Division of Criminal Justice Services. Accessed March 19, 2016. http://www.criminaljustice.ny.gov/crimnet/ojsa/initiatives/offender_reentry.htm.

Offender Reentry Task Force Initiative. Accessed March 19, 2016. http://www.criminaljustice.ny.gov/crimnet/ojsa/initiatives/offender_reentry_cospecific.htm.

Open Book New York. 2014. Office of the New York State. http://wwe2.osc.state.ny.us/transparency/contracts/contractresults.cfm?ID=1556693. Comptroller. Accessed November 15, 2015.

Pager, Devah. 2007. *Marked: Race, Crime, and Finding Work in an Era of Mass Incarceration.* Chicago: University of Chicago Press.

Price, Joshua. 2008. "Participatory Research as Disruptive? A Report on a Conflict in Social Science Paradigms at a Criminal Justice Agency Promoting Alternatives to Incarceration." *Contemporary Justice Review* 11 (4): 387–412.

Price, Joshua. 2015. *Prison and Social Death.* New Brunswick, NJ: Rutgers University Press.

Reiman, Jeffrey. 2012. *The Rich Get Richer and the Poor Get Prison.* Washington, DC: Pearson.

Rethinking Reentry. 2012. "NY DOCCS Moves Toward Supervising Parolees by Risk Level." *Re-thinking Reentry*, 28 February. http://rethinkingreentry.blogspot.com/2012/02/ny-doccs-moves-toward-supervising.html. Accessed June 26, 2016.

Robinson, Gwen, Fergus McNeill, and Shadd Maruna. 2013. "Punishment in Society: The Improbable Persistence of Probation and Other Community Sanctions and Measures." In *The SAGE Handbook of Punishment and Society*, edited by Jonathan Simon and Richard Sparks. London: Sage, 321–40.

Sentencing Project. 2016. "U.S. Prison Population Trends 1999–2014: Broad Variation Among States in Recent Years." Last modified February 16, 2016. http://sentencingproject.org/doc/publications/inc_US_Prison_Population_Trends_1999-2014.pdf.

Simon, Jonathan. 1988. "The Ideological Effects of Actuarial Practices." *Law and Society Review* 22: 771–800.

Sitrin, Marina. 2006. *Horizontalism: Voices of Popular Power in Argentina.* Oakland: AK Press.

Temporary Assistance Source Book/New York State Office of Temporary and Disability Assistance. Last modified 2011. http://otda.ny.gov/programs/temporary-assistance/tasb.pdf. Accessed June 26, 2016.

Walker, Joseph. 2013. "State Parole Boards Use Software to Decide Which Inmates to Release." *Wall Street Journal*, October 11.

Wacquant, Loïc. 2010. "Prisoner Reentry as Myth and Ceremony." *Dialectical Anthropology* 34: 605–20.

Chapter 5

Is This What Decarceration Looks Like? Rising Jail Incarceration in Upstate New York

Andrew J. Pragacz

Despite[1] sustained decarceration in New York State as a whole, mass incarceration persists in communities outside New York City and its suburbs, or in "upstate" New York (henceforth "upstate").[2] Unlike the rest of New York, upstate has not retreated from carceral forms of punishment. In 2014, upstate New York relied more on jails (which hold people awaiting court action and those sentenced to terms of one year or less) and prisons (institutions housing people convicted of crimes and sentenced to terms longer than one year) than in the past. From 1999 to 2014, when decarceration took place statewide as prison populations fell from their peak, average daily jail populations in upstate New York increased by 22 percent.[3] The number of people consigned to state prisons from upstate communities also grew by 17 percent over that time period.[4] The changes are so drastic that upstate New York now accounts for a disproportionate share of people committed to state prison and the state's jail population.[5]

These observations prompt a stark conclusion: upstate is not decarcerating. Declines in total statewide incarceration hide a reconfiguring of the state's uneven carceral geography, dividing downstate and upstate, and urban and rural. Jail incarceration upstate is an alarming counter-trend to decarceration in New York State that points to the limits of decarceration for social justice goals, namely restricting, and for some eliminating, punitive custodial confinement. This chapter argues that interactions among county criminal justice systems and state and federal governments encouraged, and assisted in expanding jail capacity and the use of jails. This approach contrasts with existing jail studies that use individual jails as their unit of analysis, employing county specific explanations (Carmichael 2005; Herkimer County 2006, 2011; Klofas 1987, 1990), or study jails by type (i.e., size) and ignore regional relationships (Ruddell and Mays 2006). National jail studies for their part similarly fail to capture much less explain carceral expansion.

DEVOLUTION: STATE DECARCERATION, LOCAL INCARCERATION

Twenty years of institutional and policy realignment have led New York State and the federal government to rely increasingly on counties and municipalities to manage incarcerated people. County governments have become convenient junior partners upon which state and federal governments offload political and economic liabilities and costs. If and when cost savings for the state and/or federal government arise, savings will stem from any transfer of costs to counties and localities.[6]

Complicated relationships among local, state, and federal agencies result in increased jail incarceration through what Miller (2014) calls "carceral devolution." Miller (2014) uses the term to capture the "set of interrelated policies that transfer carceral authority . . . from federal and state-based institutions to local ones" and corresponding shifts in rehabilitative logic (308). Decarceration promotes a double offloading: states move rehabilitation "outside prison walls" (ibid.) into "disadvantaged communities . . . of poor people" (314) and, in turn, service agencies shift moral accountability for success or failure onto poor people.

The federated nature of the US carceral state enables carceral devolution by spreading law enforcement, the management of people convicted of a crime, and costs out between various layers of government. In this system local actors have enormous power in how they apply, interpret, and wield law (Ball 2014; Lynch 2011; Black 1971), even as official policy and law making authority remains largely in the hands of state and federal officials. Carceral devolution, however, is not a singular process, but a trend within the criminal justice system with numerous facets, as this collection shows. In New York State three moments of carceral devolution have promoted jail incarceration: state-level changes in drug sentencing laws enacted in 2009, New York State's oversight power of jails and prisons vested in the State Commission of Corrections (SCOC), and the federal expansion of policing powers. These three moments, detailed below, work together to produce oversized jails and over-incarceration.

This discussion of upstate jailing confronts distinct patterns of incarceration within upstate. Counties with fewer than 250,000 people in upstate New York[7] saw the biggest increases in combined jail and prison incarceration, while the four largest urban centers of upstate taken together saw declines. Surprisingly, the smallest, most rural counties are driving jail and prison incarceration in upstate. Outcomes differ between downstate and urbanized upstate counties, and the rest of the state for at least three reasons. Smaller upstate counties have limited resources to facilitate expanded use of alternatives to incarceration (ATI), more punitive criminal justice systems, and are, by definition, located far away from major metropolitan centers. These features of small county criminal justice systems, when faced with processes of carceral devolution, produce increased use of jails.

While the media and scholars have written extensively on state prisons, jails actually incarcerate more people within a given year, making jails central to the problems of mass incarceration and, consequently, decarceration. Through the period of mass incarceration, the number of people in jail and prison, respectively, quadrupled.[8] Jail and prison incarceration grew together, along with every other piece of the US criminal justice system. The average daily population (ADP) of US jails is half of the US prison population, but high jail turnover means over 11 million people were incarcerated in jails in 2014 (Minton and Zheng 2014, 8) compared to less than 2.8 million that directly experienced prison incarceration.[9]

Jails are also sites of tremendous social injustice. Most people residing in US jails have not been convicted of a crime (Minton and Zeng 2015). Many are incarcerated simply because they cannot afford to pay bail (Subramanian, et al. 2015; Petteruti and Walsh 2008). Persons incarcerated in jails are also three times more likely to commit suicide than those in prison (Chammah and Meagher 2015). Jails also contain fewer and poorer services, from health to education (Kerle 1998, 117–46; Price 2015). Even short stints in the county jail have serious consequences, resulting in the loss of employment, housing, and relationships with dependent family members (New York Civil Liberties Union 2014). People experiencing jail incarceration often find it more punitive than prison (May, et al. 2013).

While the parallel growth of jail and prison populations suggest they are closely related, a shift to decarceration appears to be delinking these growth patterns. Decarceration potentially leads to "trans-institutionalization" similar to that experienced with the deinstitutionalization of mentally ill people in the 1960s and 1970s, whereby homeless shelters, sidewalks, relative's homes, jails, prisons, and nursing homes replaced mental health hospitals and asylums (Lamb and Bachrach 2001; Metzl 2009, 133–36). As other chapters in this volume detail, programing provided by nonprofit organizations and policing are now substituting for prisons in the era of decarceration. Moreover, decarceration not only holds out the prospect of replacing prisons with in-community surveillance, but for "*trans*-incarceration" (Petersilia and Cullen 2015, 21), where incarceration in jails becomes even more commonplace even while imprisonment in state institutions becomes less so.

The place of jail incarceration is elemental to strategies to reduce prison populations. Proponents of criminal justice reform are quick to point out that imprisonment is expensive (American Legislative Exchange 2015), socially unjust (Alexander 2011), and does not produce benefits, like reduced crime, corresponding with its human and fiscal costs (Jacobson 2005, 106–30). Reform proponents propose "smart on crime" initiatives, including expanded ATI programs, specialty courts (McLeod 2013), reduced sentences (Clear and Austin 2009), and parole reform (Jacobson 2005, 131–72). For any of these solutions to be effective in reducing prison incarceration, however, requires the cooperation of locally based community corrections that feature jails as central institutions. When probation or parole is revoked or one falters in an ATI program or court ordered treatment, jail is often the consequence. Similarly, the result of arrests stemming from intense police surveillance and coordination is, again, jail. Rather than simply "ascendant policing . . . supplant[ing] incarceration" (McQuade, this volume), we may see *both* more incarceration in jails and intensified surveillance as a consequence of decarceration.

That fact that scholars and reformers have paid relatively little attention to jails and jailing is unsurprising, given their often isolated, local nature and the poor populations they house. In New York State, as elsewhere, jails are run and paid for by counties or large cities. Most often operated by the county sheriffs, jails tend to hold local people arrested by local police for mundane low-level offenses (Greenberg and Rosenheck 2008; Petteruti and Walsh 2008; Subramanian, et al. 2015). People incarcerated in jails are also the most politically, economically, and socially disadvantaged groups within a community, eliciting little sympathy from the broader public (Irwin 1985). When scholars do examine jails, the large jail complexes of world cities like New York take center stage (Applegate and Sitren 2008; Carmichael 2004; Irwin 1985; Wacquant 2002).

Assessing the prospects of decarceration requires detailing to what extent state imprisonment is being traded for in-community sanctions, and at the center of community corrections stands the jail. So far, policy makers and activists have understood decarceration as the process of diminishing imprisonment in state-run institutions. In order to comprehend and evaluate decarceration, however, activist and policy makers must extend their vision to jails and other forms of prison-like surveillance. The promise of decarceration will not be met until criminal justice surveillance is diminished as a whole. With this in mind, the next section sketches the empirical outlines of jail and prison incarceration and their differing uses by geographic location in New York State. As an early implementer of decarceration, New York, and its uneven carceral geography, exemplifies the pitfalls of decarceration.

NEW YORK'S UNEVEN CARCERAL GEOGRAPHY

The carceral geography of the state is being reconfigured as jail and prison incarceration expands for upstate residents and is reduced for inhabitants of New York City and its suburbs. For over forty years the transfer of people of color from downstate to upstate prisons located in rural, white towns defined incarceration in New York, producing the current connotation in the phrase "going upstate." Today these flows are shifting as upstate New York sends ever greater numbers into state prisons and especially county jails. Adding further complexity, larger urban areas upstate with significant populations of people of color, including Albany and Buffalo, are sending fewer people to jail.

The numbers tell the story: in 1999 there were approximately 9,100 people sitting in upstate jails on any given day; by 2014 there were over 11,000. Over the same time period, upstate New York's crime rate fell and population remained steady.[10] The story for New York City's massive jail system provides a sharp contrast: by 2014 the jail's population was less than half its 1991 peak, hovering under 10,000 (SCOC 2015). Surrounding urban jails also housed fewer incarcerated people, with Long Island shedding almost 20 percent of its incarcerated population over the same period.

Similar trends persist for imprisonment: Downstate counties sent 11,000 fewer people to state prison in 2014 than 1999, while upstate sent almost 900

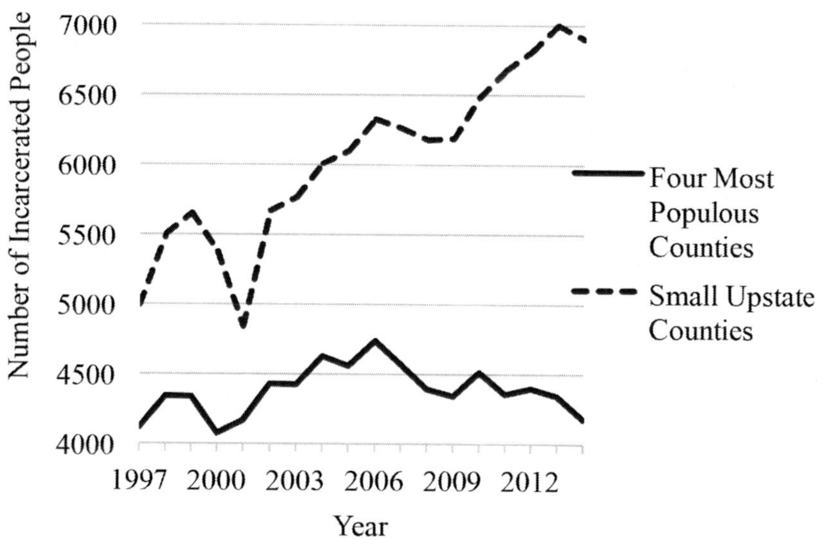

Figure 5.1 Jail Incarceration in Upstate New York, 1997–2014. *Source*: Data from "Jail Population by County: Beginning 1997" data set. https://data.ny.gov/.

more. In 1999, 73 percent of people committed to state prison came from downstate, the rest from upstate. Fifteen years later, upstate sends 45 percent of newly committed people. If new prison commitments remained the same today as in 1999, 8,279 fewer people would have been sent to state prison over the last fifteen years from upstate.[11]

By the 2000s, old models positing a "deadly symbiosis" (Wacquant 2001) between large city ghettos and upstate rural prisons no longer reflect incarceration patterns (if they ever did [Eason 2012]) as big city numbers declined, and, especially, rural upstate numbers increased. This pattern fits with recent scholarship that documents higher growth rates in jail incarceration for small and medium-sized counties across the US compared to large counties (Subramanian, Hendrichson, and Kang-Brown 2015). In the last twenty years, forty-three of fifty upstate counties' jail populations rose, with a collection of sparsely populated counties more than doubling their jail counts. Infrastructural capacity has followed increased county jail populations as small, old and often decrepit facilities were replaced during the 1990s. Between 1995 and 2004, 3,600 jail beds were added in upstate alone and an additional 2,800 beds were in some stage of planning or construction (Kaplan 2007). Currently, the neighboring counties of Broome, Cortland, and Tompkins are building or expanding jail facilities (Blakinger 2014). All said, since 1995

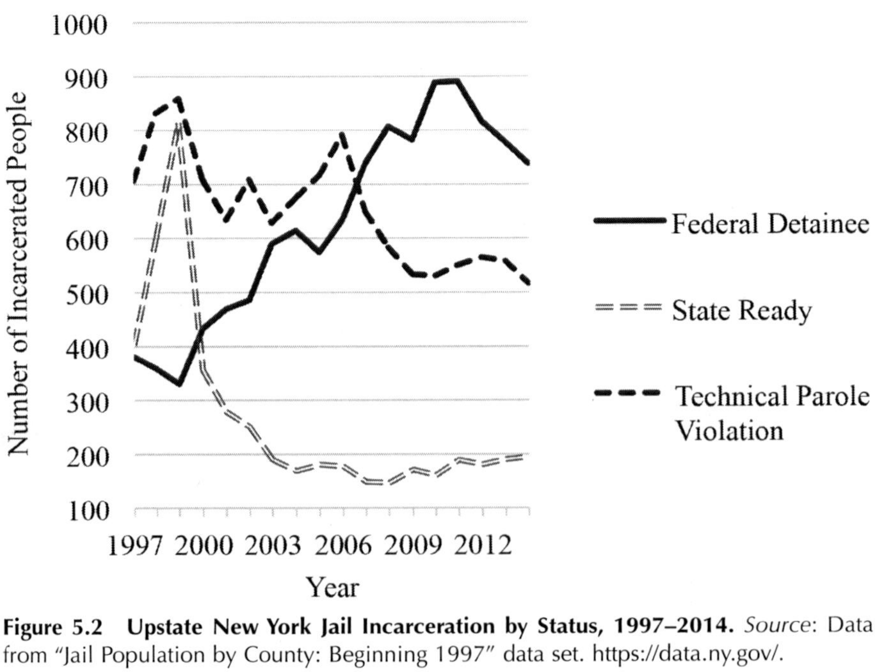

Figure 5.2 Upstate New York Jail Incarceration by Status, 1997–2014. *Source*: Data from "Jail Population by County: Beginning 1997" data set. https://data.ny.gov/.

at least thirty of upstate New York's fifty-two counties have built new jail facilities (Kaplan 2007).

Who is jailed has also changed, with upstate jails incarcerating more people awaiting trial. In 1997 48 percent of people incarcerated in upstate jails were unconvicted;[12] by 2014 the number spiked to 60 percent. Overall jail growth was only checked by the falling number of sentenced people, a population that declined by 12 percent from 1997 to 2014. Sentenced people are now outnumbered by unconvicted people, even in counties where total jail population has fallen.

Jail census trends in upstate also reveal changing relationships among local jails, state prisons, and federal policing agencies. Fewer people under state authority are occupying jail beds, as the number of parole violators and sentenced people awaiting transfer to state prisons has declined. This has been offset by jails holding more people for other counties and the federal government. Federal detainees in local upstate jails account for 18 percent of the total growth in upstate jail populations, 1997 to 2014. Incarcerated people are routinely boarded in from counties whose facilities have failed to keep pace with rising jail populations or have populations they are unable to imprison due to requirements that women and men, minors, and people awaiting sentencing must be legally held separately (Simons and Benjamin 2011, 2).

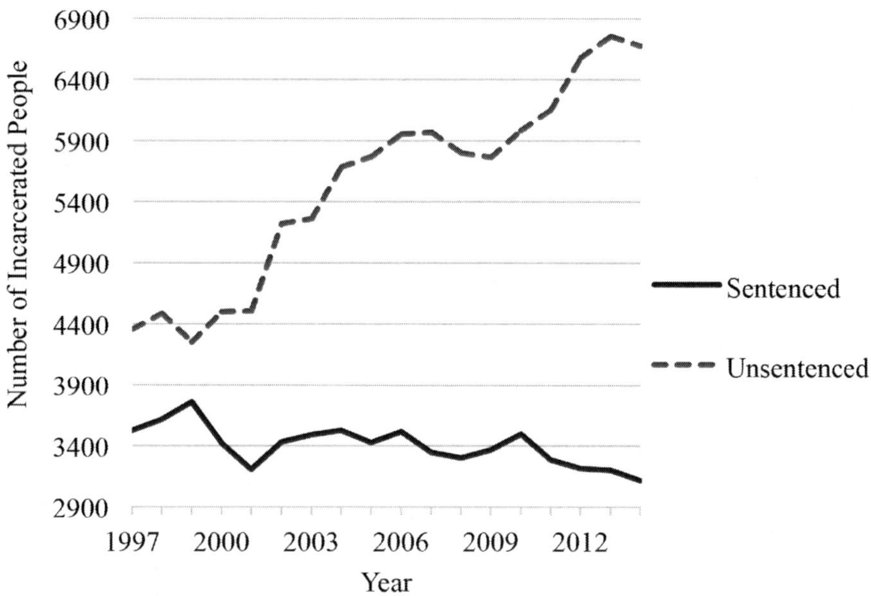

Figure 5.3 Upstate New York Jail Incarceration by Sentenced and Unsentenced, 1997–2014. *Source*: "Jail Population by County: Beginning 1997" https://data.ny.gov/Public-Safety/Jail-Population-By-County-Beginning-1997/nymx-kgkn.

At present, incarceration in New York State is thus not *just* a big city problem. The smaller counties of upstate New York that appeared to sit out the war on drugs, except for hosting prisons, are now heavily committed to incarcerating local residents. The next three sections detail three moments of carceral devolution that are driving incarceration in upstate New York, beginning with changes to sentencing laws in 2009.

SENTENCING REFORM AND EXPANDED JAIL INCARCERATION

Several unexpected developments account for the expanded jail incarceration in the upstate region. Contrary to almost all expectations, the Rockefeller Drug Law Reform of 2009 encouraged jail and to a lesser extent prison incarceration in less urbanized areas even as it helped drive down prison incarceration statewide. Enacted after decades of political challenges from criminal justice reformers, civil rights advocates, and activism by poor communities of color downstate, sentencing reforms have sought to roll back the worst injustices stemming from the harsh drug laws of the 1970s. Along with this success came another: the law succeeding in pushing people convicted of a drug crime into institutions of community corrections (like jails), in both upstate and downstate. A resurgent rural drug war upstate (but not downstate), however, increased the flow of persons into the criminal justice system in the small counties of upstate. The positive changes associated with decarceration, namely decreases in the number of new people sent to state prison in general and for drug crimes in particular, are limited to the New York City area and the larger urban centers of upstate New York.

The reforms achieve several progressive goals. First, they reduce the mandatory prison terms for some categories of non-violent drug crimes. The law also provides for alternative sentences beside prison sentences, including a six month stay in a shock incarceration facility, supervised parole coupled with drug treatment, jail, probation, or judicial diversion (Parson, et al. 201, 7). Second, the law returns judicial discretion in the matter of sentencing, a long time demand of reformers and judges alike. Whereas circumventing mandatory minimums in the past required prosecutorial agreement, under the new Reform law agreement from the prosecution is no longer mandatory (ibid.). This last piece is important to the law overall, as the increasing power afforded to prosecutors has been linked to mass imprisonment (Weiman and Weiss 2009, 83). Downstate New York exemplifies the positive changes. From 2008, the year prior to the Drug Law's enactment, to 2014 New York City sent 1,100 fewer people to state prison for drug convictions, a 46 percent decline.[13] The rest of downstate experienced an even greater decline,

63 percent, and the largest upstate counties also saw an impressive drop of 36 percent. Daily jail populations also dropped for downstate and urban upstate centers, as previously noted.

The 2009 reforms, however, fostered jail incarceration in less populous counties for three reasons. First, the law's "focus on treatment, not punishment" (Office of the Governor of New York State 2009, 1) and reduction of sentences removed drug offenders from the care of the state to counties. These changes altered which layer of government is responsible for carrying out the treatment and/or punishment: the state or a sub-state entity, like counties and cities. Embedded within the framework of a federated carceral state, localities have an incentive to send any and all offenders to prison, and onto the state's balance sheet. This is what John Pfaff (2015) dubs "budgetary moral hazard." When counties send people to state prison, those counties do not pay for that individual's incarceration, giving counties little economic incentive to incarcerate parsimoniously. From the state's budgetary standpoint moving offender management onto counties makes economic sense: ATI programs are not just cheaper than imprisonment and do not compromise public safety when properly funded (Subramanian and Moreno 2014) but they are paid for largely through county budgets with some state aid.

At the same time as counties were less able to transfer people convicted of drug crimes into state custody, a new upstate drug war led to increasing arrests, resulting in a strain on county resources and enhanced jail incarceration. In small counties there have been large jumps in felony and misdemeanor drug arrests, while the rest of upstate experienced declines.[14] The increasing drug arrests in upstate New York point to the movement of the US's long war on drugs to rural spaces (see Linneman and Kurtz 2014). Through the 2000s a moral panic over meth use washed across the state (Revier, this volume) and in recent years concerns over heroin have dominated crime reporting in upstate but also nationally. The spikes in drug arrests, in part, reflect policies that devote resources toward the policing of drugs in small towns and more rural areas, such as Operation IMPACT (McQuade, this volume).

More people convicted of drug crimes are serving sentences in communities, including jails, after the sentencing reforms. As arrests for drug crimes in the small counties of upstate increased, the number of people committed to state prison for drug crimes was flat.[15] The gap between increasing arrests and stable prison commitments means that more people convicted of drug crimes are remaining under the supervision of county and city institutions, from jails to judicial diversion. New York City successfully translated declining drug arrests and more diversion to treatment into less jail and prison incarceration. In the small counties of upstate, however, drug arrests—both felony and misdemeanor—far outpaced the number of people sent to state prisons. Furthermore, since the implementation of sentencing reform, the likelihood of being sent to prison once arrested for a drug crime fell across the board.[16] With a greater flow of persons entering the criminal justice system and less ability to offload people convicted of crimes onto the state, more people ended up under supervision of the county. Reduced sentences meant more people convicted of felony drug offenses were sentenced to jail, in and outside of New York City, after the reforms (Division of Criminal Justice Services 2011, 2012). Again, however, a reduced flow of person into the New York City criminal justice system did not lead to higher jail populations. In this sense, the law was entirely successful insofar as it pushed people convicted of drug crimes onto counties in rural upstate.

Second, upstate courts are much more punitive than downstate courts as shown by higher indictment and prison commitment rates, and the outcomes of judicial diversion programs. Indictment and prison commitment rates in the rural counties of New York dwarf those in the rest of the state.[17] For example, in 2014 New York State courts indicted four of ten people arrested for a felony drug charge. In New York City the rates were lower with three in ten people arrested being indicted. The more rural areas of upstate New York indicted people 64 percent of the time. Additionally, of people indicted for a drug crime, those in rural upstate are over three times more likely to receive a prison sentence.[18]

The treatment options provided by the 2009 Reforms, like court order treatment, are also applied more punitively. A Vera Institute of Justice report found that the reform in New York City "was not only used to divert more people [from jail and prison] but also to extend diversion to treatment to offenders with higher needs" (Parson, et al. 2015, 8). Furthermore, those people charged for a crime *eligible for diversion*, but who were not diverted, received prison and jail sentences less often (compared to before 2009) (ibid.). Meanwhile, upstate drug courts have higher non-completion rates, admit people with lesser criminal histories, and are more likely to admit people for alcoholism than New York City, *and have worse outcomes* (Cissner 2013, 30, 55; Division of Criminal Justice Statistics 2013, 12). People who fail drug court often end up in jail, meaning that high failure rates result in more jail incarceration (Division of Criminal Justice Services 2013, 12–13). Drug courts in upstate do not reduce re-arrest rates despite the fact that their risk of reoffending are much lower.[19] Even worse, by bringing in lower level offenders into the criminal justice system judicial diversion programs manifest the worst fears of reformers come true by "unnecessarily expanding criminal surveillance, diminishing procedural protections, and potentially increasing incarceration" (McLeod 2012, 1591; also see Austin and Krisburg 1982).

Finally, the reforms also failed to deliver the community investments required for a successful turn in criminal justice to community corrections

(Vera Institute of Justice 2013). State funds for treatment were slow in arriving to providers (Riggs, et al. 2014, 3) and resources are concentrated in downstate communities, disadvantaging rural spaces. The same holds for ATI program funding.[20] In a recent announcement by the Governor's office of a $5 million investment in ATI throughout the state, only $372,000 went to areas outside major urban centers (Office of the Governor of New York State 2014).

Sentencing reform did have one major outcome: it pushed offenders and costs downward to the county level. Small upstate counties met the challenge of scarce resources, an intensified war on drugs, and a diminished ability to send offenders to state prison by relying even more on jail incarceration to manage drug offenders.[21]

THE STATE COMMISSION OF CORRECTIONS

Sentencing reform was but one force propelling increasing incarceration in local jails. Even prior to the 2009 sentencing reforms, new jail beds were constructed throughout upstate. Another driver is the SCOC whose mandate to ensure the security, safety, and humaneness of jails in New York State. The Commission however has proven to be an effective driver of jail expansion throughout rural counties. Confronted with an aggressive organ of the state, counties are routinely forced to build jail capacity against their own wishes. Since 1995 thousands of jail beds have been added (Kaplan 2008). Upstate jail overcrowding, increasing jail incarceration, and additional capacity feedback on each other: overcrowding engenders calls for additional capacity, once online new space is quickly filled, overcrowding follows and produces new calls for further jail expansions. By the early 1990s, overcrowding—a problem in New York State jails going back to the 1980s (SCOC 1981)—generated construction of additional jail beds. Once beds have a tendency to fill. Without more beds, more jail incarceration would not be possible in New York State. On a national scale, for example, jail capacity and use rose together (Minton, et al. 2015, 3).

The "build it and they will come" phenomena is evident throughout rural upstate. Studies commissioned by counties and independent researchers find no correlation between arrests, population, and crime (Simons and Benjamin 2011, 4; Broome County 2008, 56–69; Chemung County Executive and Legislature 2005, iv; Steuben County Legislature 2006, vii; Herkimer County 2006, 2011; Kaplan 2007). The lack of any obvious correlations led one study to conclude that "capacity is driving the number of inmates at the correctional facility" (Broome County 2008, 57). In the new Essex County Jail's inaugural year in 2007, for example, its daily jail population jumped to 62 from 34 the previous year. Allegany County's numbers similarly jumped in 2008, from 63 in the previous year to 117.

The Steuben County Jail provides another good example: "Built in 1933, the earlier jail's population had almost doubled sixty years after it opened, cresting as high as 90 inmates. . . . But less than ten years after the new jail opened [in 1995], its population has increased by 50 percent, jumping to more than 150 inmates" (Perham 2004b). Despite concerns by county officials that "additional space might be too easily filled by judges and town justices more ready to sentence offenders to jail if the space is available" (ibid.), the county added over a hundred beds to the facility in 2008 to alleviate overcrowding. That year, the facility's ADP jumped by forty-four persons, led by increases in federal detainees. Since then, the population has remained relatively stable, in part due to investments in ATI programs (Perham 2004a). This example, however, leaves unsettled the mechanisms by which how new capacity raises jail population.

Overcrowding is produced, in part, by particularities of local criminal justice operations. One academic report on jailing in the Hudson Valley region of New York State concluded that "county jail usage is subject to choices within the county criminal justice system, and is therefore amenable to local intervention" (Simons and Benjamin 2011, 4). Simply put, judges and prosecutors fill additional jail space. A survey of New York State judges found that extra jail "detention bed space [had] a significant impact on the number of defendants released pretrial. Participant [judges] in jurisdictions with recently constructed jails reported that few defendants [were] released pending trial" while overcrowded jail conditions produced the opposite effect (Crime and Justice Institute 2014, 8). Prosecutors also use jailing as a method of extracting plea deals, which in turn leaves people unconvicted of any crime filling jail beds (Steuben County Legislature 2005, vi). This tactic would not be possible without the infrastructural capacity for it.

In its current form, the SCOC is meant to ensure the safety and accountability of carceral facilities in the state. The commission is legally responsible for overseeing all carceral facilities in the state and insuring that each facility meets state standards on population segregation, accommodations, the care and treatment of incarcerate people, and grievance procedures. It also reviews complaints submitted by incarcerated people and inspects county jails and lock-ups regularly. Established in 1985, the SCOC's mission and autonomy were expanded in the 1970s as the civil rights and prisoner's rights movements led to dramatic changes in how prisons were operated and who was incarcerated (Jacobs 1980; Meuiner and Schwartz 1973; Gottschalk 2006). The extension of civil rights to incarcerated people forced systemic change throughout the prisons systems, most notably those systems' bureaucratization—in the Weberian sense (Weber 1978, 956–1005). As one New

York State commission noted: "It is no longer possible for any Correctional system to ignore the constitutional and legal rights of the inmates under its jurisdiction" (McGinnis, quoted in Meuiner and Schwartz 1973, 941). The SCOC was subsequently reoriented to provide professionalized oversight: "the Commission's mission is to provide for a safe, stable, and humane correctional system and for the delivery of services therein" (New York State Commission of Corrections 2008, 4). While attempts at humanitarian reform took place within New York State, those changes proved compatible with the unprecedented period of mass imprisonment.

SCOC's mission to promote humane incarceration now encourages new jail expansion. This was not always the case. During the 1980s, the Commission interpreted its mandate to address overcrowding by advocating for systemic change in the criminal justice system. A 1981 Commission report on overcrowding in "local correctional facilities" called for legislative changes far outside its explicit mandate (New York State Commission of Corrections 1981, ii). To alleviate overcrowding it called for new construction, decriminalization of unspecified "behaviors now considered criminal," sentencing reform, laws governing "pre-adjudicatory detention," and more ATI programs (ibid.). While New York State tackled overcrowding in the state prison system by building prisons, no statewide plan emerged to meet the challenge of jail overcrowding. By the 1990s SCOC took it upon itself to force counties to construct new, larger jails. Since then, the Commission has cut back its prison inspection operations (Office of the New York State Comptroller 2008) and today it devotes the majority of its time and resources to monitoring local and county carceral facilities. With this shift of focus, it began to aggressively push counties to build or expand jails in order to comply with state standards.

To foster new jail construction, the SCOC developed a program "to provide technical assistance to counties undergoing expansion" (Kaplan 2007, 5), and by 2014 ten of upstate New York's counties were involved (New York State Commission of Corrections 2014, 42–43). As Kaplan (2007) notes "since the creation of this program, the SCOC has been responsible for mandating the size and timetable of nearly every new jail project in New York State" (5). The SCOC has a number of sticks to apply to counties unwilling to acquiesce to demands for new construction. Once the SCOC determines that a facility is either outdated or overcrowded, they often revoke variances for facilities out of compliance with state standards. Recently, one county legislator summarized his county's interaction with SCOC saying, "I can't understand why New York State is closing jails [sic], but is forcing us to build (quoted in Juteau 2011b)."

The SCOC has also provided political cover for elected sheriffs to expand capacity when new, costly construction engenders significant resistance.

As several SCOC watchers have noted (e.g., Simons and Benjamin 2011; Kaplan 2007), the SCOC fails to consider factors outside jail walls that may contribute to jail incarceration. The only solution offered to overcrowding, no matter the cause, is infrastructure expansion.

The long battle of rural Herkimer County with SCOC is instructive in understanding SCOC's forceful advocacy of jail construction. The Herkimer County Jail was originally built in 1978 to hold approximately forty people a day and in 1990 was holding forty-one. By 2014 the Herkimer County Sheriff's Department was, however, responsible for incarcerating eighty-three people, with the majority boarded out to another county's jail. The main driver of the ADP, according to a report commissioned by Herkimer County, was pretrial detention, which "was more than four times higher in 2009 than 1990" (Herkimer 2011, 13). The report urged the County to explore alternatives to incarceration which would limit jail capacity needs. The SCOC chose otherwise, pushing the county to build a large, 130-bed, $33 million facility near the outskirts of town (Landcastle 2015). This would replace, SCOC argued, an outdated, inefficient, and deteriorating facility (Beilein 2011). The local Sherriff agreed, calling the current facility labor intensive and expensive (Kellett 2011).

The SCOC used its ability to determine jail capacity and control variances to effectively mandate the building of a new jail in Herkimer. While SCOC consistently points out it "does not have the authority to compel any county to build a new facility" (Beilein 2011), its actions demonstrate that it does have the power and patience to make non-compliance expensive. Frustrated with the county's lack of progress, SCOC reduced or threatened to reduce the jail's authorized capacity several times, which would have burdened the county with extensive financial costs (Neely 2006; Juteau and Sorrell-White 2010; Juteau 2011a). Each time the county responded by taking steps in build a new facility, once by approving $19 million in bonding for new jail construction (Juteau 2011c). As of January 2016 the jail was still not under construction.

The only reason a new jail has remained unbuilt is intense local opposition to the project. Like other places across upstate, the forced construction of a new jail was vigorously opposed. Jail expansion has, unlike prison expansion (Fitchen 1991, 215–25), met with regular, broad resistance from county residents and elected officials. Since jails are funded by local taxes, they are likely to face resistance by local taxpayers, as opposed to prisons which are funded by the state and are often welcomed by distressed communities.

The fight was led by a group of fiscally conservative property owners under the name Concerned Citizens for A Better Herkimer County (CCBHC) and the Herkimer City Council. Opponents of the jail penned their own report

(CCBHC 2006), arguing that housing people out to other facilities was cheaper than building a new facility and challenging SCOC's assessment of the facility as "crumbling" (CCBHC 2006, 12). Several members were elected to the Legislature itself on just this issue. The City of Herkimer passed a zoning resolution designed to prevent the jail's construction within city limits, where the county sought to place it.

FEDERAL POLICING AND LOCAL JAILS

The expansion of federal policing power through "the criminalization and localization of immigration enforcement" (Gottschalk 2015, 228) has also pushed infrastructure and population expansion for jails. Beginning in the early 1990s, the federal government turned to local policing authorities to curb illegal immigration. Acts passed in 1996 gave local police the power to enforce immigration law (Provine and Varsanyi 2012, 106). After 9/11, the federal government sought to turn jails into detention and information-gathering sites through the Secure Communities program. Under that program every person booked into a county jail is automatically searched against a federal database, and if flagged for an immigration violation a detention hold can be placed on the individual, removing local discretion (Provine and Varsanyi 2012). People detained by Immigration and Customs Enforcement (ICE) occupied 2.5 percent of all jail beds on any given day in 2014, totaling over 16,000 people (Minton and Zeng 2015). Hundreds of facilities nation-wide have agreements in place to detainee undocumented people, including privately owned and operated facilities (US Immigration and Custom Enforcement 2007). Detention orders were issued against 436,000 individuals across the country in 2012 and 2013, the majority of whom had at most minor criminal convictions (Transactional Records Access Clearinghouse 2014).

As detention holds surged, ICE quickly sought to expand its carceral capacity. ICE operates few facilities itself, preferring to contract out detention to counties or private companies (US Department of Homeland Security 2009). Partly, this reflects the realities of geography: the perimeter of the US is almost 9,000 miles, over half of which is land border. This need also reflects legislative reality. Starting in 2007, ICE has incarcerated 34,000 a day on average, costing ICE over $2 billion a year (Morgenthau 2014). The logistical problem of locking up so many along the US border is massive. To manage this task ICE turned to agreements with jails and counties throughout the country to hold people for a set price to supplement construction of large new detention facilities (Buch 2014; Ruddell and Mays 2011).

Upstate New York is a prime example of these new arrangements, given its long border with Canada and its distance from any major urban center and ICE's own detention centers.

Out of the fifty-two upstate counties in New York, thirty-eight held federal detainees during the last nine years. All told, federal detainees in upstate jails almost trebled from 1997 to 2014, jumping from 4 percent to 7 percent of all jail beds, affecting thousands of individuals.

In upstate New York many rural counties constructed new facilities with the intention to fill these beds with federal detainees (CCBHC 2007). Despite some signs of resistance by the New York State Sheriff's Association (Semple 2014), entrepreneurial sheriffs view federal government outsourcing as a boost to their power and funding (Ruddell and Mays 2011). The federal government willingly helps build jails as long as infrastructural and inmate liability remains with the local county. In these arrangements the federal government offloads its responsibility and liability to counties and local governments, which have fewer procedural, pay, and hiring mandates to consider, making jailing detainees significantly cheaper. By contracting with local jails ICE gains plausible deniability for injuries caused by cost cutting, poor facilities and conditions, or lack of legal representation (MacDonald 2013; New York Civil Liberties Union 2014).

The inflationary effect on jail capacity by the surge of federal dollars is well illustrated by Clinton County's attempt to build a new jail. Clinton County occupies the northeast county of New York State, bordering Canada and Vermont, and contains two state prisons. The combination of a border location and an incarceration-based economy made Clinton County well positioned to contract with federal agencies. In 1999, with prison incarceration peaking, the county sought to pay off its ten year-old jail by adding fifty beds for the federal government (Ferrer 1999). The idea languished until after 9/11, when the influx of federal dollars turned a modest fifty bed expansion plan into a doubling of jail capacity (*Press Republican* 2002). US Marshalls Service (USMS) guaranteed it would occupy one-fourth of the new beds at $90 daily (ibid.). In addition, the Department of Homeland Security contributed $1.8 million to the jail's $24.5 million construction cost (LoTemplo 2005). The other 120 odd beds were constructed to appease SCOC demands for a bigger facility. Thanks to federal funding, the county government was able to sell the expansion to the public by highlighting federal financing and a purported crime wave (Jolly 2004). Predictably, the number of incarcerated people ballooned from 134 the year prior to the new jail's completion to 216 by 2014. While the sentenced population grew by 14 percent from 2005 to 2014, the number of federal detainees trebled to twenty eight, and the unconvicted population surged from sixty to 114 people per day. By 2014, board-ins from other counties, prophesied to bring great financial returns for the county's jail investment, shrunk to zero.

The promised use of jails by federal agencies to detain undocumented immigrants facilitated the expansion of jail across the state, acting as a means to sell large facilities to a weary, budget conscious citizenry. Yet the consequences of construction are not as straightforward. Larger facilities, as the previous section noted, tend to fill. In the case of Clinton County, while the number of federal detainees did increase after construction, the USMS did not sustain its stated carceral commitments long term, representing thousands in loss revenue for the county.[22] Furthermore, the result of increased jail capacity was not just more space for the federal government, but greatly expanded incarceration of unconvicted persons with US citizenship. The greater use of county jails by the federal government facilitated expanded levels of incarceration for all persons, and not just undocumented people.

CONCLUSION

Jail incarceration in the small counties of upstate New York has been driven by local forces interacting with state and federal criminal justice agencies. The devolution of incarceration to local counties and their new jails was not foreordained. Without the state's oversight commitment to new jail construction, non-carceral options could have been adopted even before the heroin and meth scares. In turn, the promise of federal funds to offset the fiscal costs of supersized jail construction projects facilitated meeting SCOC's demands. This has been not a single process of devolution, but multiple overlapping processes that produce more jail incarceration.

What does this research say about the prospects of decarceration? First, it highlights decarceration as a spatially uneven process, one that may reduce incarceration in one place, but increase it in others. Second, if decarceration is to succeed in meeting its social justice promises beyond prison walls, scholars and activists need to turn attentions to jails. And third, left unchecked, other institutions of the criminal justice system will grow to compensate for decarceration, sustaining and reproducing monitoring of people charged and/or convicted of crimes under prison-like conditions.

These warnings extend to the future of New York's jails. Increasingly, popular opinion has shifted away from "tough on crime" policies. This softening, however, is rapidly being reduced to what Kilgore (2014) terms "carceral humanism," with jails being cast as rehabilitative and treatment spaces. The risk is real that resources devoted to abating the problems of drug addiction and mental health will flow to jails. Future jails may well be sold as therapeutic spaces. To prevent future jail expansion and jail incarceration, communities need to decommission jail space and invest resources outside the criminal process system.

NOTES

1. This piece is dedicated to the Broome County Legislature. In early 2014, Broome County decided to expand its jail. A small group of us meeting regularly as the Binghamton Justice Project decided to oppose the expansion. Brendan McQuade and I presented data—some of which is presented in this piece—at the Legislature's Public Safety and Emergency Services Committee that, to our minds, undermined the expansionist argument. The Committee humored us for those few minutes, but would not permit us to present our case to the Legislature the following week. Instead, we protested with fliers, information, and banners. As the expansion plan passed by a wide margin, a group of 20 or so stormed out, booing. Besides infiltrating photos of the County's Executive's State of the County Address with our signage, we accomplished little else at the time. Experiencing the Legislature's intense opposition to factual claims about jail incarceration and their intense commitment to incarceration first hand, I set out to investigate jailing across the upstate New York. I would like to thank every member of the Decarceration Working Group at Binghamton University: Luis González, Chungse Jung, William Martin, Joshua Price, and Kevin Revier. Also thanks to Reuben Miller. Special thanks to William Martin and Josh Price for their invaluable mentoring and prudent editorship.

2. Definitions of upstate New York vary. For the purpose of this chapter "downstate" is composed of New York City and its suburbs, including Long Island, Westchester, Putnam, Orange, Dutchess, and Rockland Counties. Anything in New York State but outside of "downstate" is considered "upstate." Phrases like "mostly rural areas of upstate New York," "less urbanized spaces of upstate New York" and "small upstate New York counties" refer to counties with populations under 250,000 people. This follows Subramanian, Henrichson, and Kang-Brown's (2015) nationwide jail survey wherein counties with 250,000 people or fewer are categorized as "small counties." This chapter also uses the term "most urbanized counties" to mean the four most populous counties within upstate, Albany, Erie, Monroe, and Ononodaga.

3. All statistics on jailing outside New York City were retrieved from Open Data New York (https://data.ny.gov/), unless otherwise noted. All jail and prison populations are reported as ADPs, which reflects the average number of people held in a facility over the course of a year.

4. All prison commitment data was provided by the New York State Department of Corrections and Community Supervision. For commitment data by county for the years 2006 to 2013 see the yearly reports found at http://www.doccs.ny.gov/Research/annotate.html#pop. For 2014 see https://data.ny.gov/.

5. The 2010 census puts New York State population at 19.3 million people. Approximately 32 percent of those, or 6.3 million, live in upstate. In 2013, 13,694 people were sent to New York State prisons from all counties. Upstate sent 5,804, or 41 percent. Similarly, the ADP of New York State jails in 2014 was 27,571. Upstate's share was 11,078, or 40 percent.

6. As Martin (this volume) notes the costs associated with decarceration are hard to pin down. Savings from decarceration are associated with reducing prisons and prison staff. But when this is done the work of managing "criminal offenders" does not end, but is transferred presumably with some of the costs.

7. See Note 2 above.

8. See table 6.14.2012, http://www.albany.edu/sourcebook/pdf/t6142012.pdf and 6.28.2012, http://www.albany.edu/sourcebook/pdf/t6282012.pdf from University at Albany, Hindelang Criminal Justice Research Center, *Sourcebook of Criminal Justice Statistics*. Accessed June 27, 2016.

9. I found no estimates of how many individual people experience prison incarceration directly within a given year that accounts for admissions, releases, and those who remain incarcerated during the entire year. In 2014, 644,000 people were admitted to US prisons and 636,000 people were released (Carson 2015). Adding admitted, released, and ADP together yields an impossibly high estimate of 2,824,515 people that directly experienced prison incarceration in 2014. This number does not necessarily reflect how many people were actually incarcerated in prison over 2014, but is an upper limit on how many could have possibly been incarcerated in prison that year.

10. Crime and population data acquired from https://data.ny.gov/.

11. "Statistical Overview Year 1999 Court Commitments," Department of Corrections and Community Supervision (author files obtained through a Freedom of Information Law request). "Prison Admissions: Beginning 2008" obtainable at https://data.ny.gov/Public-Safety/Prison-Admissions-Beginning-2008/m2rg-xjan. Retrieved June 27, 2016.

12. Available statistics categorize people as either "sentenced" or "unsentenced." The latter term includes people "awaiting arraignment, trial, awaiting sentencing by the court, or are Parole Violators with New Arrests" (DJCS 2016). The vast majority of people, however, are not convicted of crime since the number of people who have been convicted of a crime but are not yet sentenced is very low. Acknowledging this fact, a recent report from the Subramanian, et al. (2015) uses unconvicted person when describing people termed unsentenced by the Bureau of Justice Statistics (5).

13. All of the statistics on felony drug commitments, indictments, and arrests in this section, unless otherwise noted, are derived from numbers provided in the Division of Criminal Justice Services annual report on the Rockefeller drug laws (Division of Criminal Justice Services 2015).

14. Arrests rates for felony and misdemeanors in small counties grew 18 percent and 46 percent respectively from 2008 to 2014. Felony drug arrests statewide fell by 31 percent and misdemeanors by 20 percent.

15. In 2008 1,068 people were sentenced from upstate to state prison compared to 1,101 in 2014.

16. Statewide, the likelihood of being sentenced to prison for a felony drug crime fell from 13 percent to 12 percent, 2008 to 2014, and the small upstate counties' rate dropped from 31 percent to 27 percent.

17. A large majority of indictments—the act of being formally charged with a crime—result in some form of sentence, most likely through plea bargaining (see Division of Criminal Justice Services 2011).

18. Someone arrested for a drug crime in the small counties of upstate has a 26 percent chance of being sent to prison in 2014 compared to 8 percent in New York City. https://data.ny.gov/Public-Safety/Adult-Arrests-by-County-Beginning-1970/rikd-mt35.

19. I should note that evidence from New York City is also mixed. It was found that those "who were eligible for diversion were still more likely to receive a custodial sentence than [to] be diverted to treatment" (Parsons, et al. 2015, 15).

20. For a full list of state supported ATI programs see http://www.criminaljustice.ny.gov/opca/ati_directory.htm.

21. The probation rolls outside the major urban centers fell, as might be expected given declining overall arrests. Despite increasing arrests for drug offenses, however, incidents of probation for drug felonies fell by 8 percent and increased by only 8 percent for misdemeanor drug offenses, far below percent increase in drug arrests.

22. USMS promised to hold at least thirty-six persons a day in the Clinton facility (LoTemplo 2004). While they achieved that goal and more in four out of nine years from 2006 to 2014, the number of detainees dropped to twenty eight by 2014.

REFERENCES

Alexander, Michelle. 2010. *The New Jim Crow: Mass Incarceration in the Age of Colorblindness*. New York: New Press.

American Legislative Exchange. 2015. "Recidivism Reduction: Community-Based Supervision Alternatives to Incarceration." *The State Factor*: 1–12. Retrieved November 10, 2015, http://alec.org/docs/Recidivism-Reduction.pdf.

Applegate, Brandon K. and Alicia Sitren. 2008. "The Jail and the Community: Comparing Jails in Urban and Rural Contexts." *The Prison Journal* 88 (2): 252–69.

Austin, J. and B. Krisberg. 1982. "Unmet Promise of Alternatives to Incarceration." *Crime and Delinquency* 28(3): 374–409.

Austin, James and Michael Jacobson. 2013. "How New York City Reduced Mass Incarceration: A Model For Change?" Vera Institute of Justice: New York. Retrieved November 10, 2015, http://www.vera.org/pubs/how-new-york-city-reduced-mass-incarceration.

Ball, David W. 2014. "Defunding State Prison." *Criminal Law Bulletin* 50 (50): 1060–90.

Beilein, Thomas A. 2011. "Guest View: Regional Jails an Answer, but Challenging." *Utica Observer-Dispatch*, February 12. Retrieved November 10, 2015, http://www.uticaod.com/article/20110212/NEWS/302129934.

Black, Donald J. "The Social Organization of Arrest." *Stanford Law Review* 23 (6): 1087–111.

Blakinger, Keri. 2014. "Tompkins County Jail Expansion: The Murky Reasons for Spending $900k." *Ithaca.com*, March 14. Retrieved November 10, 2015, http://www.ithaca.com/news/tompkins-county-jail-expansion-the-murky-reasons-for-spending-k/article_07b5c87a-a9df-11e3–842c-0019bb2963f4.html.

Broome County. 2008. "Final Report: Study of the Broome County Sheriff's Department." Prepared by Voorhis/Robertson Justice Services, Inc. Retrieved March 22, 2016, http://www.gobroomecounty.com/files/legis/08_1007_Final%20Broome%20Report%20Total.pdf.

Buch, Jason. 2014. "Critics Frown at ICE Jail Contracts." *San Antonio Express-News*. Retrieved November 10, 2015, http://www.expressnews.com/news/local/article/Critics-frown-at-ICE-jail-contracts-5817099.php.

Carmichael, Jason T. 2005. "The Determinants of Jail Use Across Large US Cities: An Assessment of Racial, Ethnic, and Economic Threat Explanations." *Social Science Research* 34: 538–69.

Carson, E. Ann. 2014. "Prisoners in 2013." Bureau of Justice Statistics.

———. 2015. "Prisoners in 2014." Bureau of Justice Statistics.

CCBH (Concerned Citizens for a Better Herkimer County). 2007. "Jail Report: Evaluations & Recommendations." Prepared by Joseph Chilelli.

Chammah, Maurice and Tom Meagher. 2015. "Why Jails Have More Suicides than Prison." The Marshall Project. Retrieved March 22, 2016, https://www.themarshallproject.org/2015/08/04/why-jails-have-more-suicides-than-prisons#.7B02bigJR.

Chemung County Executive and Legislature. 2006. "Strengthening Criminal Justice System Practices in Chemung County, NY." Prepared by the Center for Governmental Research Inc.

Cissner, Amanda B., Michael Rempel, and Allyson Walker Franklin. 2013. "A Statewide Evaluation of New York's Adult Drug Courts." New York: Center for Court Innovation.

Clear, Todd R. and James Austin. 2009. "Reducing Mass Incarceration: Implications of the Iron Law of Prison Populations." *Harvard Law & Policy Review* 3: 307–24.

Crime and Justice Institute. 2014. "Assessment of Pretrial Services in New York State." Prepared for the New York State Association of Pretrial Service Agencies and the New York City Criminal Justice Agency. Boston: Crime and Justice Institute.

Division of Criminal Justice Services. 2011. "2009 Drug Law Update." Retrieved March 22, 2016, http://criminaljustice.ny.gov/drug-law-reform/documents/drug-law-reform-presentation-print-jun2011.pdf.

———. 2012. "2009 Drug Law Update." Retrieved March 22, 2016, http://criminaljustice.ny.gov/drug-law-reform/documents/drug-law-reform-june-2012.pdf.

———. 2015. "2009 Drug Law Changes, 2015 Annual Report." Retrieved March 22, 2016, http://criminaljustice.ny.gov/crimnet/ojsa/FINAL-2015-DLR-Update.pdf.

———. 2016. "Jail Population Outside New York City by Month." Accessed June 26, 2016, http://www.criminaljustice.ny.gov/crimnet/ojsa/jail_population.pdf.

Dyer, Joel. 2000. *The Perpetual Prisoner Machine: How America Profits from Crime.* Boulder, CO: Westview Press.

Ferrer, Saul G. 1999. "County Seeks Grants to Expand Jail." *Press-Republican (Plattsburgh, NY)*, September 19.

Fitchen, Janet M. *Endangered Spaces, Enduring Places: Change, Identity, and Survival in Rural America.* Boulder, CO: Westview Press.

Greenberg, Greg A. and Robert A. Rosenheck. 2008. "Jail Incarceration, Homelessness, and Mental Health: A National Study." *Psychiatric Services* 59 (2): 170–77.

Gottschalk, Marie. 2006. *The Prison and the Gallos: The Politics of Mass Incarceration in America.* New York: Cambridge University Press.

_____. 2014. *Caught: The Prison and the Lockdown of American Politics.* Princeton, NJ: Princeton University Press.

Herkimer County. 2006. "Updated Jail Population Analysis." Prepared by LaBella Associates.

_____. 2011. "Jail Projections Update: Herkimer County, New York." Prepared by CRS Inc.

Irwin, John. 1985. *The Jail: Managing the Underclass in American Society*. Berkeley: University of California Press.

Jacobson, Michael. *How to Reduce Crime and End Mass Incarceration: Downsizing Prisons*. New York: New York University Press.

Jolly, Anna. 2004. "State Analysis Says Clinton County Jail Understaffed." *Press-Republican (Plattsburgh, NY)*, June 28.

Juteau, Rob. 2011a. "State Commission Opts Not to Renew Jail Variance." *The Evening Times* (Little Falls, NY), January 26.

———. 2011b. "Bonding for Jail OK'd." *The Evening Times* (Little Falls, NY), February 11.

———. 2011c. "Lawmakers Want to Continue to Collect Additional Sales Tax Funds." *The Evening Times* (Little Falls, NY), April 7.

Juteau, Rob and Stephanie Sorrell-White. 2010. "Commission Gives County 30 Days to Show Progress." *The Evening Times* (Little Falls, NY), October 29.

Kaplan, Dana. 2007. "Impacts of Jail Expansion in New York State: A Hidden Burden." New York: Center for Constitutional Rights.

Kellett, Linda. 2011. "Farber Fields Questions on New Jail." *The Evening Times* (Little Falls, NY), May 6

Kerle, Kenneth E. 1998. *American Jails: Looking to the Future*. Boston: Butterworth-Heinemann.

Kilgore, James. 2014. "Repackaging Mass Incarceration." *Counterpunch*. Retrieved March 22, 2016, http://www.counterpunch.org/2014/06/06/repackaging-mass-incarceration/.

Klofas, John. 1987. "Patterns of Jail Use." *Journal of Criminal Justice* 15: 403–11.

———. 1990. "Measuring Jail Use: A Comparative Analysis of Local Corrections." *Journal of Research in Crime & Delinquency* 27 (3): 295–317.

Lamb, Richard H. and Leona L. Bachrach. 2001. "Some Perspectives on Deinstitutionalization." *Psychiatric Services* 52 (8), 1039–45.

Landcastle, Rebecca. 2015. "Herkimer County Jail Stalemate Putting Chains on Progress." *Utica Observer-Dispatch*, August 23. Retrieved February 15, 2016, http://www.uticaod.com/article/20150823/NEWS/150829798.

Linnemann, Travis and Don L. Kurtz. 2014. "Beyond the Ghetto: Police Power, Methamphetamine and the Rural War on Drugs." *Critical Criminology* 22 (3): 339–55.

LoTemplo, Joe. 2005. "Historic Upgrade—Sheriff Sees Revenue in Jail Epxansion." *Press-Republican (Plattsburgh, NY)*, January 15.

Lynch, Mona. 2011. "Mass Incarceration, Legal Change, and Locale." *Criminology & Public Policy* 10 (3): 673–98.

MacDonald, Robin. 2013. "ACLU Calls for Investigation, Closure of Georgia Immigrant Dentention Centers." *Daily Reporter*. Retrieved March 22, 2016, http://www.acluga.org/news/2014/03/26/aclu-calls-investigation-closure-georgia-immigrant-detention.

Mauer, Marc and Nazgol Ghandnoosh. 2014. "Fewer Prisoners, Less Crime: A Tale of Three States." The Sentencing Project. Washington, DC.

May, David C., Brandon K. Applegate, Rick Ruddell, and Peter B. Wood. 2014. "Going to Jail Sucks (and it Really Doesn't Matter Who you Ask)." *American Journal of Criminal Justice* 39 (2): 250–66.

McLeod, Allegra M. 2012. "Decarceration Courts: Possibilities and Perils of a Shifting Criminal Law." *The Georgetown Law Journal*, 100: 1587–1674.

Metzl, Jonathan. 2009. *The Protest Psychosis*. Boston: Beacon Press.

Meuiner, Paul D. and Howard D. Schwartz. 1973. "Beyond Attica: Prison Reform in New York State, 1971–1973." *Cornell Law Review* 58 (5): 924–1034.

Miller, Reuben Jonathan. 2014. "Devolving the Carceral State: Race, Prisoner Reentry, and the Micropolitics of Urban Poverty Management." *Punishment & Society*, 16 (3): 305–35.

Minton, Todd D., Scott Ginder, Susan M. Brumbaugh, Hope Smiley-McDonald, and Harley Rohloff. 2015. "Census of Jails: Population Changes, 1999–2013." Washington, DC: Bureau of Justice Statistics.

Minton, Todd D. and Zhen Zeng. 2014. "Jail Imates at Midyear 2013." Washington, DC: Bureau of Justice Statistics.

———. 2015. "Jail Imates at Midyear 2014." Washington, DC: Bureau of Justice Statistics.

Morgenthau, Robert M. 2014. "The US Keeps 34,000 Immigrants in Detention Each Day Simply to Meet a Quota." *The Nation*, August 13. Retrieved November 10, 2015, http://www.thenation.com/article/us-keeps-34000-immigrants-detention-each-day-simply-meet-quota/.

Neely, Larry. 2006. "Commission Gives County Reprieve on Jail." *The Evening Times* (Little Falls, NY), July 14.

New York Civil Liberties Union. 2014a. "State of Injustice: How New York State Turns its Back on the Right to Counsel for the Poor." Retrieved February 1, 2016, http://www.nyclu.org/files/publications/nyclu_hh_report_FINAL.pdf.

New York Civil Liberties Union. 2014b. "Testimony Regarding Immigration Detainers." Retrieved March 22, 2016, http://www.nyclu.org/content/testimony-regarding-immigration-detainers.

New York State Commission of Corrections. 1981. "An Analysis of the Findings of the Study on the Increasing Population in Local Correctional Facilities and Some Strategies to Reduce Overcrowding."

———. 2008. "New York State Commission of Corrections Annual Report." Retrieved November 10, 2015, http://www.scoc.ny.gov/pdfdocs/annualreport_2008.pdf.

———. 2014. "New York State Commission of Corrections Annual Report." Retrieved November 10, 2015, http://www.scoc.ny.gov/pdfdocs/annualreport_2014.pdf.

———. 2016. "Inmate Population Statistics." Retrieved March 20, 2016, http://www.scoc.ny.gov/pop.htm.

Office of the Governor of New York State. 2009. "Governor Patterson Signs Rockefeller Drug Reform into Law." Retrieved March 22, 2016, http://www.communityalternatives.org/pdf/2009DLRA-Legislative-History-Governor-Press-Stmnt.pdf.

_____. 2014. "Governor Cuomo Announces More than $5 Million for Programs Designed to Reduce Crime and Change Offender Behavior." Retrieved November

10, 2015, https://www.governor.ny.gov/news/governor-cuomo-announces-more-5-million-programs-designed-reduce-crime-and-change-offender.

Office of the New York State Comptroller. 2008. "New York State Commission of Correction: Oversight of Correctional Facilities and Handling of Grievances and Complaints." Retrieved March 22, 2016, https://osc.state.ny.us/audits/allaudits/093008/06s93.pdf.

Parsons, Jim, Qing Wei, Christian Henrichson, Ernest Drucker, and Jennifer Trone. 2015. "End of an Era? The Impact of Drug Law Reform in New York City." New York: Vera Institute of Justice.

Perham, Mary. 2004a. "Programs Saved Taxpayers Nearly $3.2 Million." *Leader* (Corning, NY), February 5.

———. 2004b. "Legislators: Fiscal Woes a Roadblock." *Leader* (Corning, NY), May 16.

Petersilia, Joan and Francis T. Cullen. 2015. "Liberal But Not Stupid: Meeting the Promise of Downsizing Prisons." *Stanford Journal of Criminal Law and Policy* 2 (1): 1–43.

Petteruti, Amanda and Nastassia Walsh. 2008. *Jailing Communities: The Impact of Jail Expansion and Effective Public Safety Strategies*. Justice Policy Institute.

Pfaff, John F. 2015. "Federal Sentencing in the States: Some Thoughts on Federal Grants and State Imprisonment." *Hasting Law Journal* 66: 1567–1600.

Press Republican (Plattsburgh, NY). 2002. "Jail Expansion Only Way to Go." July 30.

Price, Joshua. 2015. *Prison and Social Death.* New Brunswick, NJ: Rutgers University Press.

Provine, Doris and Monica W. Varsanyi. 2012. "Scaled Down: Perspectives on State and Local Creation and Enforcement of Immigration Law." *Law & Policy* 34 (2): 105–12.

Riggs, Robert, Jim Parsons, Qing Wei, and Ernest Drucker. 2014. "From Punishment to Treatment: A Providers Perspective on the Implementation of 2009 Rockefeller Drug Law Reforms in New York State." *Health & Justice* 2 (10): 1–14.

Ruddell, Rick and G. Larry Mays. 2006. "Expand or Expire: Jails in Rural America." *Corrections Compendium* 31 (6): 1–5.

———. 2011. "Trouble in the Heartland: Challenges Confronting Rural Jails." *International Journal of Rural Criminology* 1 (1): 105–31.

Semple, Kirk. 2014. "New York State Sheriffs Shying Away from Immigration Detention." *New York Times*, July 30. Retrieved November 10, 2015, http://www.nytimes.com/2014/07/31/nyregion/new-york-state-sheriffs-shying-away-from-immigration-detention-.html?_r=0.

Simon, Joshua and Gerald Benjamin. 2011. "A Collaborative Approach to County Jailing in the Hudson Valley." New Paltz, NY: Center for Research, Regional Education, and Outreach.

Steuben County Legislature. 2005. "Strengthening Alternatives to Incarceration Programs and Criminal Justice System Practices in Steuben County." Prepared by the Center for Governmental Research Inc.

Subramanian, Ram and Rebecka Moreno. 2014. "Drug War Détente? A Review of State Level Drug Law Reform, 2009–2013." New York: Vera Institute of Justice.

Subramanian, Ram, Christian Henrichson, and Jacob Kang-Brown. 2015. "In Our Own Backyard: Confronting Growth and Disparities in American Jails." New York: Vera Institute of Justice.

Subramanian, Ram, Ruth Delany, Stephen Roberts, Nancy Fishman, and Peggy McGarry. 2015. "Incarceration's Front Door: The Misuse of Jails In America."

Transactional Records Access Clearinghouse. 2014. "Targeting of ICE Detainers Varies Widely by State and by Facility." Accessed March 30, 2016, http://trac.syr.edu/immigration/reports/343/.

US Department of Homeland Security. Office of the Inspector General. 2009. "Immigration and Custom Enforcement Detention Bedspace Management." Washington, DC.

US Immigration and Custom Enforcement. 2007. "U.S. Immigration and Customs Enforcement Office of Detention and Removal Operations Semiannual Report on Compliance with ICE National Detention Standards January–June 2007." Washington, DC.

Wacquant, Loïc. 2001. "Deadly Symbiosis When Ghetto and Prison Meet and Mesh." *Punishment & Society* 3 (1): 95–133.

———. 2002. "The Curious Eclipse of Prison Ethnography in the Age of Mass Incarceration." *Ethnography* 3 (4): 371–97.

Weber, Max. *Economy and Society Volume II.* Edited by Guenther Roth and Claus Wittich. Berkeley, CA: University of California Press.

Weiman, David and Christopher Weiss. 2009. "The Origins of Mass Incarceration in New York State: The Rockefeller Drug Laws and Local War on Drugs." In *Do Prisons Make Us Safer? The Benefits and Costs of the Prison Boom*, edited by Steven Raphael and Michael A. Stoll, pp. 73–116. New York: Russell Sage Foundation.

Williams, Marian. 2003. "The Effect of Pretrial Detention on Imprisonment Decisions." *Criminal Justice Review* 28 (2): 299–316.

Conclusion

A New Reconstruction?

Joshua M. Price and William G. Martin

Each year since 2000, nearly 700,000 people on average are released from state or federal prisons. If we include those released from jails, the number grows substantially. For comparison's sake, nearly 4 million people were freed from slavery at the end of the Civil War. Every day, advocates and activists propose new changes to the criminal justice system. For the first time in decades, we can hear an echo of those calls for reform, albeit weak and qualified, among mainstream politicians, foundations, philanthropists, pundits, and journalists. Given the record levels of incarceration, even incremental changes in the inmate population will result in unprecedented numbers of people released. If even some of the policy proposals are enacted, in other words, if even a few more prisons close, then the current torrent will seem only a trickle.

Yet one of the peculiarities of the current moment is how this shift in the mainstream conversation about criminal justice and the actual decline in the prison population, as dramatic as it has been, had not been predicted by many criminologists. Advocates against mass incarceration also failed to foresee this turn. This book has tried to wrestle with the underlying and precipitating causes of decarceration, gauge its magnitude, and trace its consequences. This new phase should be cause for guarded optimism. We are potentially on the cusp of a social transformation of a scale we have not seen since Reconstruction.

ON THE CONDITIONS FOR FREEDOM

Comparisons between prisons and slavery can be overdrawn. Similarly, it would be overhasty to make too much of any symmetry between emancipation and prison abolition. In any case, on a practical level it would make little sense: the United States still incarcerates more people than any nation, and it would be hard to argue that *that* will end any time soon.

But the parallels are suggestive. As with Reconstruction, decarceration implies not merely the prospect of a racialized subject population sprung free of their fetters. Decarceration offers a broader political opening that can potentially remake groups across racial hierarchies. Reconstruction posed fundamental political, economic, social, and even psychological challenges, and so does decarceration. And then there is the sobering thought that Reconstruction failed. It was defeated by the forces of white supremacy and the interests of property.

How can we learn the lessons from the past?

Those freed today, as in the past, emerge relatively unprotected from the potential predations of the larger society. People who leave prison have been isolated and institutionally humiliated. Their family and communal ties have been rent; and as a group they have few resources and almost no political power. Their civil rights are restricted, sometimes permanently. Many suffer from a poor education. They may have substance abuse issues or mental health problems—a disproportionate number do. They are set adrift in a rapacious, highly individualistic, and competitive capitalist society. Their predicament is compounded if one thinks of the institutional and interpersonal racism many face.

The challenges of reentry are not borne by them alone, but rather shared by kin, peers, and entire communities. Communities of color have endured patterns of residential segregation that have only increased in the past forty years. Unemployment is rife, especially in poor communities and communities of color; the formerly incarcerated have a particularly tough row to hoe. The infrastructure for treating mental illness and substance abuse is inadequate.

This is not to paint newly freed persons and their home communities as helpless, passive, or as damaged goods. This is not to portray them as simply victims (and one must move beyond the dichotomy of innocent victim/cruel perpetrator). It is not to exculpate them from any harm they have done. Instead, it is to point to all the social and structural ways they reenter at a significant disadvantage.

What is the nature of the freedom that they face?

In liberal theory, liberty is sometimes defined as the absence of constraints or barriers. But this is an anemic sense of liberty on at least two counts. First, it defines liberty in purely negative terms: to be free is to be free from obstacles, such as government intervention in one's life (Berlin 1958). It says little about the positive conditions that must obtain to make that liberty more than an abstraction. To be free in a robust sense means to have those conditions that can make that life flourish. W. E. B. Du Bois noticed a similar problem with the "freedom" offered to black people during Reconstruction. They were free from chattel slavery, but they were thrown unprepared into a new society, largely without the education, civil rights, or the political wherewithal to resist organized attempts to disenfranchise them socially, politically, and economically (Du Bois 1935, 130, 184).

What are the social and material conditions for the possibility of freedom? This is a practical question, requiring a concrete, non-utopian response. Freedom is not a given, in the abstract and in negative terms. It requires the transformation of central pillars of the old order: the courts and the law as they uphold a racial caste system in an officially colorblind society, the police as its occupying army. The reorganization of education with equal access to all, housing as a human right, social services for those in need, and civic rights guaranteed for all must follow as well. We must insist on deep cultural changes to move us away from stigmatizing those convicted of a felony. We must find ways to deal with institutional and interpersonal injuries and violence, without turning all harmful acts into *criminal* acts with criminal consequences. These transitions entail a material transformation, a reallocation of resources, but also a conceptual shift. The prospect of freedom is demanding indeed.

Freedom, however, is not simply a question of the requisite social infrastructure for the rational pursuit of one's ends. Freedom must be leavened with justice. Reconstruction was an attempt by black people to forge new conditions of life and to realize a vision for community and society at a moment when support from the federal government existed, however momentarily and provisionally. With the defeat of Reconstruction, the forces of capital and white supremacy again disenfranchised African-Americans, and subjected them to laws and police powers that restricted their movement, the conditions in which they lived, labored, loved, and communed. Those committed to white supremacy used extra-judicial terror (the lynching bee, rape) in tandem with the law to reestablish white rule and unfettered capitalism. The growth of the convict-lease system and the imposition of the Black Codes marked a transition from the end of Reconstruction to the criminalization of people of color. One could add to this the rise of racialized immigration and naturalization laws as another element of legalized white supremacy. Together, these elements amounted to the gradual construction of an unjust infrastructure. At the same time, the defeat of Reconstruction meant the death of a certain vision of social justice. It is not too late, however, to make good on that vision.

JUSTICE DISINVESTMENT AND THE NEW INFRASTRUCTURE OF INJUSTICE

Pursuing a vision of freedom requires creating a just society. Put in negative terms, the absence of justice, and of the guarantee of justice, is not moral neutrality. It is social death. Injustice can also be expressed in positive terms, even if that injustice is hidden. From the standpoint of modern liberalism, for example, the market is imagined as just and free, since the citizen-consumer is free of encumbrances to pursue his or her ends. But this is an illusion. The infrastructure of injustice channels and burdens the racialized and gendered subject into subordination.

Beginning in 2013 and with increasing intensity in the following years, many have proclaimed that we are entering an age of criminal justice reform. The present wave of justice reform appears to anticipate a more just society. But this may be little more than a mirage that flatters the viewer. As one travels across New York, no common Zeitgeist can be found. As we comb through the post-industrial detritus of abandoned prison buildings, boot camps, and youth facilities, and compare them to the busy construction sites that will result in new jail wings in Dutchess County, in a southeast corridor of the state already replete with prisons, Broome County along the Susquehanna, or Erie County near the Canadian border, we can gather the tangible and intangible fragments of another narrative underneath, or behind, the dominant one that proclaims reform is the order of the day. While drug law reform is clearly upon us, for example, some parts of the state are going through a moral panic about heroin addiction and phantom meth labs that has recently reached the fever pitch of the crack scare of the 1980s. As the penitentiary population drops by almost a third, and prisons close downstate and upstate, the number of people in jail has swelled. At a time when New York City politicians and advocates openly debate the closing of the mammoth Riker's Island Jail in New York City, legislatures in a dozen upstate counties contemplate expanding their jails. While the state closes cruel and abusive youth prisons upstate, new and less transparent ones are born anew through subcontracts to private providers and facilities in New York City. Some parts of New York seem to be ushering in a new era of reform while others are still living an ethos of the harshest period of law and order policing. And throughout one finds greater integration and coordination by the state in policing, prisons, jails, and parole. The current moment, in short, is full of ironies and puzzles. The future we face appears to be neither emancipatory reform nor simply the continuation of past mass incarceration.

We advance the term *justice disinvestment* to unpack and explain these conundrums. The concept of justice disinvestment emerges from the snapshots provided in the previous chapters. It designates a fitful and still uncertain attempt to develop a criminal justice regime less reliant on the prison and yet potentially far more expansive and pervasive. For example, intelligence-led policing is not merely a new policing technique or even just another attempt by law enforcement agencies to facilitate the flow of information. Instead, intelligence-led policing has moved into the very mechanisms of the state administrative process as it manages knowledge, social space, and populations. Brendan McQuade describes this process as the emergence of a new Leviathan. Not only are police involved, but also civilians are persuaded and prodded into complicity. Landlords and police collude in "zero-tolerance" leases. People swept up in police nets are pressured to "debrief" or inform. Probation and parole offices use risk-assessment tools and the police utilize CompStat and other data-driven programs to facilitate interagency collaboration that identifies risky individuals, neighborhoods, or tenants.

Hobbes' Leviathan, it will be recalled, was formed by a social contract, in which members alienated certain rights to a powerful sovereign. The figure of the contract has become modern liberalism's conceit to describe the origins of society. This social contract, as Carole Pateman and Charles W. Mills have argued, contains an implicit sexual and racial contract. So, too, does the new Leviathan contain an implicit discourse about racial and sexual subordination. This embedded process is part-and-parcel of statecraft for the racialized state.

> The state's management of racial categories is analogous to the management of highways or ports or telecommunication: racist ideological and material practices are infrastructure that needs to be updated, upgraded, and modernized periodically: this is what is meant by racialization. (Gilmore and Gilmore 2013, 144)

The injustice does not emanate only from the state but becomes part of deeper and wider social and cultural phenomena. Chapter 2 describes a drug scare fanned by upstate newspapers. The panic over meth labs that the newspapers generated in New York's secondary and tertiary cities thrives symbiotically with new forms of policing such that the agents of vigilance and law enforcement come to include not just the police but also shopkeepers, landlords, and teachers. The insecurity spreads out from the state into the social and cultural fabric of the society and back again.

This is arguably an American tradition that reaches back through the lynch mobs to Salem. The police work with everyday people and whatever media and communications technology exist to scapegoat and persecute a racialized or gendered other. In its most recent avatar, online newspapers, Twitter, Instagram, Facebook, messaging software, and public safety mobile phone applications allow for moral panics to erupt in rural and urban America, and the stigmatized—the meth cooks, the sex offenders, and the like—become the subject of overheated, racialized newspaper campaigns of fear and vengeance that can work hand-in-glove with police in a positive feedback mechanism.

We can similarly celebrate the closing of prisons only to find they are counterbalanced or compensated in part by new forms of county and municipal surveillance and an uptick in incarceration in jails. And while ex-prison towns face a bleak future, those released from their prisons face not freedom but social death ensured by the devolution of reentry, supervision, and support services to private sector firms and nonprofit organizations.

In these cases, the state has relinquished to the private and nonprofit sector its responsibility to administer justice while coordinating and imposing greater management, supervision, and surveillance of the formerly incarcerated and their communities. The outcome is reentry and reform without liberty and justice. Put in positive terms, carceral devolution is justice disinvestment.

An apparent retreat by the state may satisfy some libertarians, but in this case state retraction in certain spheres comes with an expansion of its management and monitoring capacity in others. These conditions maximize the exposure of the formerly incarcerated to the vagaries of a difficult labor market on the one hand (Purser 2012) and the reassertion of nativism and racism on the other. The result is that subaltern groups are released without the positive resources to make freedom meaningful. Greater social justice is not gained, but denied.

What is gained is an infrastructure of injustice. To read across each of the previous chapters generates this disturbing prospect of systemic change, but not, or not yet, for the better. What if the reform is for the worse? Each of the previous chapters designates a spoke in a wheel, jails, policing, reentry, drug scares, and the transformation of prison towns. If one were to focus only on a spoke, one loses a sense of the whole, just as one would get a myopic view of decarceration by focusing only on New York City. No common ideology or discourse is needed for this new paradigm to take hold. In fact, the right cocktail of ideological diversity across the state (and the country) may help usher in justice disinvestment.

Many of the countervailing attempts at reinvestment are in effect more justice disinvestment. The reentry task forces, undertaken in the name of community wellbeing and public safety, ensnare the formerly incarcerated in a baroque net of services providers, law enforcement, and sundry other community organizations. The state has refused to construct or reconstruct communities and neighborhoods that have been decimated and preyed upon by decades of aggressive policing and mass incarceration. A project of construction or reconstruction of communities also implies reconstructing social relationships.

Although we should not depend on the state as guarantor of justice, the state bears a special responsibility. It is the state, after all, that imprisons people and confers what Devah Pager (2009) calls the negative credential of a criminal record. This negative credential makes it so hard for formerly incarcerated persons to find employment, education, and housing, regain custody, or, in the case of immigrants—makes it so difficult to attain citizenship or even stay in the country, as well as all the other myriad ways in which the formerly incarcerated experience an ongoing civil and social death.

A "just" state—a state committed to justice—may be a contradiction in terms. Indeed, in conferring responsibility to the state alone, an active public may be implicitly abjuring its own responsibility; we all bear responsibility for ensuring justice in the families, workplaces and communities in which we live. In order to realize the promise of what Du Bois called an abolition democracy, an active public must hold the state accountable while struggling to develop safe housing, employment, and material wellbeing for *all* who need it, to develop, in short, those elements for a just society, one whose institutions do not monitor endlessly, systematically humiliate, or commit systematic violence.

If there is no effective arbiter for justice, especially for vulnerable people, then the society is effectively unjust. Abnegation by a citizen or an institution is an abnegation of responsibility. Although we are enlisted, by newspapers, by the police, by the schools, into vigilance on behalf of the state, we can instead substitute a just set of aims.

REFERENCES

Berlin, Isaiah. 1958. "Two Concepts of Liberty." In *Four Essays on Liberty*, pp. 118–72. Oxford: Oxford University Press.

Du Bois, W. E. B. 1979 (c.1935). *Black Reconstruction in America; an Essay Toward a History of the Part Which Black Folk Played in the Attempt to Reconstruct Democracy in America, 1860–1880.* New York: Atheneum.

Gilmore, Ruth Wilson and Craig Gilmore. 2013. "Restating the Obvious." In *Indefensible Space: The Architecture of the National Insecurity State*, edited by Michael Sorkin, pp. 141–63. New York: Routledge.

Pager, Devah. 2009. *Marked: Race, Crime, and Finding Work in an Era of Mass Incarceration*. Chicago: University of Chicago Press.

Purser, Gretchen. 2012. "Still Doin' Time: Clamoring for Work in the Day Labor Industry." *WorkingUSA* 15 (September): 397–413.

Index

Note: Page references for figures are italicized.

About the Contributors

John Major Eason is as an Assistant Professor in the Department of Sociology at Texas A&M University. Before entering graduate school he worked as a church-based community organizer focusing on housing and criminal justice issues. He also served as a political organizer most notably for then Illinois State Senator Barack Obama. His forthcoming book (March 2017), *Big House on the Prairie: Rise of the Rural Ghetto and Prison Proliferation*, links race, punishment, and spatial inequality to community processes and political economy.

Luis R. González is pursuing a master's degree in city and regional planning at the Edward J. Bloustein School of Planning and Public Policy at Rutgers University. He serves as a graduate research assistant for the Ralph W. Voorhees Center for Civic Engagement, where his work concentrates on understanding how income and access to different modes of transportation influence food security for New Brunswick residents. Additional research interests include: transportation equity, transit's influence on gentrification, community economic development through public–private partnerships, international student mobility, and the socioeconomic repercussions of spatial inequality, as well as its causes. He received his Bachelor of Arts in Geography from Binghamton University, graduating as a McNair Scholar and Phi Beta Kappa.

Chungse Jung is a PhD Candidate of Sociology at the State University of New York at Binghamton. The working title of his dissertation is *The Age of Protest: World-Historical Structure and Dynamics of Protest Waves in the Global South, 1875-2012*. His research interests include world-historical study of social movements, media analysis of counter-hegemonic struggles, structural inequality of the World-Economy, and governance and resistance of neoliberal urbanizations in the Global South.

William G. Martin teaches at Binghamton University. His work has focused on the racial and political economy of southern Africa, New York State, and global social movements. Books include *South Africa and the World-Economy: Remaking State, Race, and Region* (2013), *From Toussaint to Tupac: The Black International since the Age of Revolution* (with Michael West and Fanon Che Wilkins 2009), and *Making Waves: Worldwide Social Movements, 1760-2005* (Coordinator 2008). He has long been a member of groups working to support incarcerated adults and youth.

Brendan McQuade (PhD, Binghamton University 2015) is an assistant professor of sociology at SUNY-Cortland. He has published on policing and intelligence in *Surveillance & Society* and *Qualitative Sociology*. His broader areas of research and writing include the critique of security, the sociology of culture and knowledge production, and the study of social movements. In the fall of 2015, he acted as the lead author of *The Counter-CAPS Report: The Community Engagement Arm of the Police State*, an independent study of community policing in Chicago conducted by members of We Charge Genocide, a Chicago-based, grassroots, intergenerational effort to amplify the voices and experiences of the young people most targeted by police violence.

Andrew J. Pragacz is a Sociology PhD student at Binghamton University. His research interest include critical criminology, world-ecology, and the sociology of work and labor. His intended dissertation topic is the Erie Canal and capitalist civilization, with an emphasis on labor control and ecological change. He is also a local social justice activist and publishes work regularly in *The People's Press* (Binghamton, NY), which he also edits.

Joshua M. Price teaches in the Sociology Department of the State University of New York at Binghamton. He writes on institutionalized racial and gender violence. He is the author of *Prison and Social Death* (2015) and *Structural Violence: Hidden Brutality in the Lives of Women* (2012). From 2004 to 2007, he directed the NAACP's Broome County (New York) Jail Health Care Project. In 2006, he co-founded the Southern Tier Social Justice Project to advocate for formerly incarcerated people. For his work, the Broome/Tioga County NAACP has honored him as Citizen of the Year and the New York State Assembly has cited him for "Outstanding Commitment to the Civil Rights of New Yorkers."

Kevin Revier is a PhD student in the department of sociology at the State University of New York at Binghamton. His research interests include: moral panic, media, and criminalization. His dissertation work is on crime news reporting and drug reform in upstate New York.